Reflections

By
ELAINE JORDAN

© **Truth Publications, Inc. 2018. Second Printing.** All rights reserved. No part of this book may be reproduced in any form without written permission from the publisher. Printed in the United States of America.

ISBN 10: 1-58427-363-1

ISBN 13: 978-1-58427-363-9

First Printing: 2012

Truth Publications, Inc.
CEI Bookstore
220 S. Marion St., Athens, AL 35611
855-492-6657
sales@truthpublications.com
www.truthbooks.com

Table of Contents

City Lights 5
Do You Believe In Sin? 7
The Awe of History 9
Troublesome Times are Here 11
My Mom's Example 15
Being a Rich Christian 17
The Pursuit of Happiness 21
Satan's Battle 25
The Pleasure of Anticipation 29
Am I Like My Father? 33
Two Men Named Ananias 35
Hypocrisy in Christians 37
Having It God's Way 41
Wishes and Hopes 45
Beacons on the Hill 49
Are You a Problem-Solver? 53
Your Shame and God's Forgiveness 55
Marco Polo 59
Losing Your Kazip 61
Meandering Fences and Creeks 65
Are You A Gladiator? 69
Dear Diary 71
"Just the facts, Ma'am" 73
Paul and the Thorn in His Flesh 77
Do As the Romans Do 81
The Third Son 83
Your Household Idols 85
Looking Into the Abyss 89
The Elephant in the Room 93
My Friend 95
Peter and Geometry 97

Author's Notes and Acknowledgements

Thank you to the many people who have inspired me and encouraged my writing. My family and friends are so special to me and every writer depends on their family and friends in so many ways.

Special thanks to my husband, Ray, for his untiring support and courage. He has read so many versions of my short essays with both praise and criticism. Every writer should be lucky to have such wonderful assistance. My sons, Adam and Scott, have actively helped me with ideas and sometimes they have such sound idea development! I am blessed to have these wonderful Christian men in my life. To all the other members of my family, thank you for your encouragement.

I have so many friends that have supported my writing. However, special thanks to Meredith Carr and Carl Witty for their help reviewing drafts of *Reflections*. Their interest, thoughtfulness, insight, and time certainly improved the content of my essays and reduced my grammatical errors.

I have used the New King James version of the Bible for my essay quotes. I hope you enjoy this translation.

Elaine Jordan
July, 2012

City Lights

Our contemporary lives are full of lights, so that even the dimmest corner is brightened with a tall fluorescent security light. Our highways are lined with streetlights to aid motorists to see other vehicles, pedestrians, obstacles, and the roadway itself. Our homes have switches at every room entrance, so we can turn on one or more lights before we enter the room. Everywhere in the cities and byways, colorful lights advertise for goods and services and also provide entertainment and information to us. These lights seem to compete with each other to get our attention. They demand – Come to my store – Buy my product – Watch my show – Turn this way to my city! City lights are such a part of our lives that we don't even think about them and expect the lights to provide many services to us.

Jesus knew humans were attracted to light and needed lamps at night in their homes and gathering places. In the Sermon on the Mount (Matt. 5:14-16), Jesus told the multitudes, *"You are the light of the world. A city that is set on a hill cannot be hidden. Nor do they light a lamp and put it under a basket, but on a lampstand, and it gives light to all who are in the house. Let your light so shine before men, that they may see your good works and glorify your Father in heaven."* Jesus knew people understood how they used light in the physical sense. People traveling at night could see the light of the city while it is a great distance away. The city lights would shine across the desert. No one in a house lights a lamp and hides it under a basket. The light was put on a stand so that everyone in the house could use the light. Using these physical examples of how a light is used in the darkness, Jesus tells Christians to be a light in the spiritual sense.

How can a Christian be *the light of the world*? Remember, Jesus is telling us to be spiritual lights. We sparkle and shine when we are *be-*

ing a Christian. Our spiritual light is evident to others as we live our everyday lives. For example, when the grocery clerk misses the sack of potatoes under the cart, a shining Christian comes back to pay for the potatoes; when our neighbor is having a hard time, a sparkling Christian mows the yard and invites the neighbor to church; when a coworker tells you no one will notice the missing work supplies, a gleaming Christian does not steal from his or her employer; when your friend asks you why you smile each day, a glowing Christian tells the friend of the hope of heaven; when an acquaintance wants you to go drinking as used to be your habit, a shimmering Christian declines the invitation. Shining Christians shows their light to the dark world when they tell others of their faith, when they perform good works, when they are a good citizen, and when they correct their own mistakes.

If the world cannot see your spiritual light, then how can you really be a Christian? A Christian in name only will be no different than anyone else. Christians must work hard to be the light of the world. This hard work is for God's glory, not the individual Christian's glory. Our light must shine in the dark world to show everyone our hope of heaven and to light our path forward to heaven. The world needs to know the reason of our hope and faith. Without our sparkling and shining spiritual lights, how will the world know about God?

Today, city lights are everywhere and it is hard to see through the brightness of our cities. Jesus is telling us that our Christian example should be as obvious! So let your light shine so the whole world can see God in you!

Do You Believe In Sin?

Do you believe in sin? I mean, do you really believe in sin? I think most people do not, because everywhere around me, I see a very coarse and self-centered society. How can sin be real when our whole society shouts the praises of crude activities and our heroes are lewd and indecent people? How can sin be real when Snooki and Lady Gaga are the role models for young girls and Charlie Sheen and Axl Rose are role models for young boys? Clearly sin is not real when we teach our children to imitate such salacious characters!

Webster's dictionary has three definitions of the word "sin." 1. Transgression of a religious or moral law. 2. Estrangement from God as a result of breaking God's law. 3. An offense, violation, fault, or error.

The word as defined in definition 3 is surely not in our current vocabulary when no one recognizes the fault or error of his actions toward another. Our popular culture is more worried about disrespect from others than any real offending issue. We are more interested in what others are doing than what we are doing or if we are doing the right things. How can sin be real, if political correctness ensures we never offend, violate, fault, or make an error against anyone? Sometimes, in order to be politically correct, the real "sinful" issue is ignored. In no way does sin exist if our President, Congress, and judges can define and clear up all moral matters for us. Matters such as homosexual marriage and abortion are just legislative and judicial issues, not sin, right?

The word as defined in definition 1 is a transgression of a religious or moral law. For this definition to be valid, a person must have a religion or moral law from which to transgress. Often we are like Viscount Melbourne when he said, "Things have come to a pretty pass when religion is allowed to invade the sphere of private life." We don't want a religious or moral code to interfere with our lives as we work hard to be successful in business and leaders in the community. It is easy to ignore God when everything is going well for us. Then, we can define a moral law for ourselves and ignore God, because we don't need religion! Sin is vague when it is a transgression of a personal moral law and different for any group defining the particular sin. People using this definition do not believe in sin.

The second definition of sin is more like the one we find in our Bible. A Biblical definition is found in 1 John 3:4. *Sin is lawlessness.* Webster is right in that sin causes us to be separated from God. We sin when we do not follow God's law and our sin causes us to be unacceptable to God. God's law is not legislated by any earthly group and is not a moving target. God's law is an eternal comprehensive body of laws and guidelines for our conduct. When you agree with this definition of sin, then you believe in sin.

Okay, you believe in sin, but do you really believe in God? If sin is breaking God's law, resulting in an estrangement from God, we should be afraid of any separation from God. Sin can allow us to drift away from God in a manner that doesn't cause any alarm. We can be so comfortable in our lives that sin and God are not priorities. When sin is treated lightly, then belief in God is not evident or the belief in God is so slight that no real faith exists. No faith—no God! Living without God is easy when we place our trust and confidence in our own abilities. We can be like the rich, young ruler in Luke 18. He wanted to be a follower of Jesus, but his riches and comfortable earthly life were more important to him than God. This young man did not truly believe in God and sin.

True belief in God is unmistakable when the believer enthusiastically seeks to do things pleasing to God. This believer understands God's law and avoids sin. A true believer knows *"all have sinned and fall short of the glory of God"* (Romans 3:23) and trusts God to forgive and forget his sins when asked for forgiveness. Belief in sin and God cannot be separated. God defined sin when He gave us His law, so our belief in God defines our belief in sin.

The Awe of History

Have you ever visited a major historical site and thought about the blood and tears under your feet or listened to long ago voices calling from the past?

During a visit to Ephesus, my son walked in the amphitheater where silversmiths once shouted that the Christians had ruined the trade for handcrafted idols of Diana. His appreciation of the courage and faith of the early Christians grew as he looked up into the theater seats towering over his head and imagined the silversmiths shaking their fists and pounding their feet.

Other friends have visited the Roman Coliseum where Christians were fed to lions or killed by gladiators for the crowd's entertainment. The anguished cries and blood of those Christians can be heard and smelled by any caring tourist as their thoughts go back to those grand days of the Roman Empire. How hard it must have been to be a Christian in Nero's time!

Any visit to Israel that begins with a trip to Bethlehem and ends at Golgotha moves Christians to vow a more perfect faith, because they see how God's love made salvation's path available for them. Standing where Mary must have stood during Jesus' crucifixion should be moving to any visitor. Walking in the footsteps of first century Christians makes Bible narratives echo in our mind and increases our understanding of the Bible stories of our youth.

I haven't been lucky enough to visit any biblical sites. I have been told that you read the Bible differently after walking in the footsteps of Jesus and other Bible heroes. Sometimes we read our Bible and don't appreciate what we are reading. The Bible story is familiar to us, but we don't grasp the fact that real people lived those stories. While it is important to understand the historical settings and culture of the people to appreciate the lessons of the story, it is more important to feel the awe of history and the breath of the people as we read our Bible. More important than feeling the awe and reality is to know the Bible is given to us to know about God. When we read our Bibles, we are learning about God and that is the most important thing of all.

You don't have to walk across the Red Sea on dry land to be thankful for God's power. You don't have to see Elijah ride into the heavens in a fiery chariot to feel amazement of God's might. You don't have to hear the jeers of the soldiers as Jesus stood in front of Pilate to recognize God's love. You don't have to see Jesus' empty tomb to know He lives. However, you have to listen with more than your ears as you hear any Bible story.

Listen with your heart to the voices from the past as they tell you what happened to them and how God lived then and lives now. Listen as the stories tell us about God and His love for them and for us. Listening with your heart lets the Bible speak to you and you can hear the people in the past tell us about God.

Our Bible stories are about real people who worked and loved and sang and cried just like we do. We have their stories so we can know more about God and how to please God. George Santayana once said, "Those who cannot remember the past are condemned to repeat it." Let the Bible voices shout from the past so you learn from them. Learn to repeat their good actions and avoid their bad actions. Our Bible was given to us so that we could know about God and believe. *"Now all these things happened to them as examples, and they were written for our admonition, upon whom the ends of the ages have come"* (1 Cor. 10:11).

We don't have to walk with Paul in the Ephesian amphitheater to believe. We can believe, because we have the Bible. Read your Bible, listen to the voices from the past, and know God is the same then and now and will be the same in the future.

Troublesome Times are Here

Have you ever wondered where God is when times are hard? Currently our country is splintered with a weak economy and polarizing politicians pitting citizen against citizen. Fathers and mothers cannot find work and struggle to care for their families. The weather pattern is severe with hurricanes and droughts. In an instant, earthquakes can destroy homes built over a lifetime and our loved ones are hurt or dead. Many of our young men and women serve valiantly overseas and come home broken to their families. Our family members and friends are sick and hurting. We want to help to make them well, but we cannot fix them ourselves. Where is God when times are hard? What do we do when our problems are crashing over our heads in thunderous waves?

I am writing this article as tornadoes have come again to North Alabama. This morning, several tore through neighborhoods and another wave of severe weather will come this evening. As the wind picks up and the hail falls, my stomach is clenched and I pray for rescue. In a broader sense, so many problems can be listed here which we cannot fix or avoid. We need God and pray to Him. Remember the line in the song, "Troublesome times are here, filling men's hearts with fear"?[1] Where is God during these troublesome times?

Isaiah spoke to the Jews in Babylonian captivity where they could not free themselves, but needed God to do that for them. *"But those who wait on the Lord shall renew their strength; They shall mount up with wings like eagles, they shall run and not be weary, They shall walk and not faint"* (Isa. 40:31). God was there for the Babylonian Jews who depended on Him for strength to endure during their troublesome times. Of course, when the problem is happening to us, it is the most major problem ever and the biggest troublesome time! Today, we

---

[1] "Jesus is Coming Soon," R.E. Winsett, 1968.

need God as much as those Jews did, but sometimes we forget just how much we need Him.

Our earthly problems remind us that life here on earth is not our goal. Our goal is life in heaven. No matter how much we wish for it to be so, this life is not meant to be perfect. God's love for us gives us our hope of heaven with Him and our endurance through troublesome times grows our faith and reliance in God.

I am not saying God is doing hard things in our lives. I am saying that earthly lives have many problems, because we are living an earthly life. For example, earth has gravity. When you fall down, gravity skins your knee or breaks your hip. For another example, God made us with free will. Some people use their free will to be good and kind, while others use their free will to be vicious, greedy, and mean. Good times and hard times are part of living an earthy life. The Bible tells us rain falls on both the good and the evil people and it is true.

Many times, the New Testament writers tell us to find joy in hard times. *"And not only that, but we also glory in tribulations, knowing that tribulation produces perseverance; and perseverance, character; and character, hope. Now hope does not disappoint, because the love of God has been poured out in our hearts by the Holy Spirit who was given to us"* (Rom. 5:3-5). In these verses, Paul assures the Roman Christians of their hope of heaven during their time of religious persecution. He tells them to rejoice in their troublesome times and boast of their future hope. Their hard time, faith, and hope produced endurance to reach for their reward of heaven. This is the same reward we have today. Our troublesome times grow our faith in God and hope of heaven, because we depend on God to help us through them.

I started this article when tornadoes threatened my home, but as I finish, the sun is shining and the birds are singing. Whether the tornadoes hit my house that day or not, God was with me to strengthen me and to help me endure the day and its consequences. His presence during the good times and the bad comforts and reassures us every day. The lines of this chorus describe the comfort of God's presence to me: "Till the storm passes over, till the thunder sounds no more, Till the clouds roll forever from the sky; Hold me fast, let me stand in the hollow of Thy hand, Keep me safe till the storm passes by."[2] When God has you in His hand, anything can be endured.

God is with us in our troublesome times, if we just ask for His help and comfort. He renews the strength of all who depend on Him as He did with the captive Jews. God helps us to run and not be weary and to walk and not faint, so we can endure troublesome times. Remember in Matthew 28:20, God tells us, *"I am with you always."*

---

[2] "Till the Storm Passes By," Mosie Lister, 1958.

My Mom's Example

I was lucky to have Nancy Laws as my mother. Her courage and faith in God taught me how to handle a tough situation. When Mom was told she had amyotrophic lateral sclerosis (ALS), she did not cry, even though she knew the disease was cruel and fatal. As ALS took away her ability to perform simple tasks, she did not complain. It was amazing how quickly her muscles lost the ability to sew, crochet, or hold a pencil. When people asked me how she was doing, I would tell them her spirit was calm and her faith was strong. I would like to tell you more about what I meant when I said that.

First, Mom had a close relationship with God. I thought I knew my mother well. But as I cared for her in the last months, I observed her faith and dependence on God. She had an enviable relationship with God that was very intimate and personal. She had not fallen back to God as last resort, because she already had a close bond with God. As Mom lost the ability to speak, I am sure He listened to the groaning of her soul. Mom was not disappointed in God because she was suffering and did not cry, "Why me?" One of her friends asked her how God could let her have this terrible disease and she replied, "Why not me?" She accepted this hardship with anticipation of her new life in heaven.

I learned to pray better while watching Mom pray. Mom's prayers were talking to a friend and it was evident that she had always prayed like that. In James 5:13, we are taught, *"Is anyone among you suffering? Let him pray."* When we earnestly pray to God, He shares our load. Even though Mom needed God to help with the weight of ALS, she also wanted support for her suffering family and prayed more for others than herself. I am sure God heard every prayer and was comforting my mom.

Mom spent a lot of her last hours showing others a path to God. She wanted all her friends and family to know God as she did and to be Christians. She was even persuasive during her eulogy, as she had requested songs and verses that spoke of her faith and asked family and friends to believe also. Mom did not want anyone to be like King Agrippa and say, *"You almost persuade me to become a Christian."* Mom truly worried about others' souls and wanted them to know God. She was a working Christian and followed the guidance in 1 Peter 4:19: *"Therefore let those who suffer according to the will of God commit their souls to Him in doing good, as to a faithful Creator."* In this verse, the word "suffer" does not mean pain and anguish, but to endure. Christians cannot show their endurance in God without an active faith demonstrated by good works.

Lastly, Mom was an example of Christian strength in adversity. Her love and faith in God never wavered. The apostle Paul also suffered many afflictions and persecutions. In 2 Corinthians 5, Paul writes how he longs to leave his earthly tent (body) and be with God in heaven. Both Mom and Paul were ready to be with God, but continued their earthly work until God called. Mom's two favorite verses were marked in every Bible she used and were written by Paul.

Philippians 4:11 – *"Not that I speak in regard to need, for I have learned in whatever state I am, to be content"*

Hebrews 13:5 – *"Let your conduct be without covetousness; be content with such things as you have. For He Himself has said, 'I will never leave you nor forsake you.'"*

As Mom's strength left her body, her faith kept her spirit strong. She knew God was with her as her body weakened and was content within herself.

So what did I learn from Mom? I learned to depend on God, to pray for what I need, to lead others to God, and to be content. ALS may have shortened my mother's life, but lessons learned from her life are still working. My goal in life is to live with a calm spirit and strong faith, so others can see God in me.

Being a Rich Christian

I realize "rich" is a matter of perspective. Even though you and I may not consider ourselves rich, someone else knows for certain we are! Even the poor people in our country are rich compared to the poor of third world countries. I do not mean to define what rich is here, but to assure most of us that we are rich. God has blessed us and we have so much. But can you be a rich Christian and still go to heaven?

Jesus often warns the rich. In the Sermon on the Mount (Luke 6), He says, *"Woe to you who are rich, for you have received your consolation."* Jesus was telling His listeners that it is a painful misfortune or a woe to be rich, because you have earthy blessings and forget the need for spiritual blessings and salvation for your soul. Jesus also taught about this danger in a parable about a rich man who built new barns to hold his wealth. After building the new barns, the rich man said to himself, *"'Soul, you have many goods laid up for many years; take your ease; eat, drink, and be merry.' But God said to him, 'Fool! This night your soul will be required of you; then whose will those things be which you have provided?"* Jesus concluded this parable with these words. *"So is he who lays up treasure for himself, and is not rich toward God"* (Luke 12:15-21). We can easily be like this rich man and be dead to God which is not a good plan.

You can be rich and also be a Christian. We must remember to those to whom God has given much, much is expected. We are clearly told the rich are expected to trust in God and not in wealth. *"Command those who are rich in this present age not to be haughty, nor to trust in uncertain riches but in the living God, who gives us richly all things to enjoy"* (1 Tim. 6:17). God does not want us to value our earthly treasures more than following Him. Our priority must be serving God, not making our next dollar.

Luke 18:18-30 is the story of the rich young ruler traveling with Jesus to Jerusalem. The young ruler's riches were very important to him and part of his personal identity. Jesus told the young man to sell his riches and give the money to the poor, because He knew the ruler loved being rich more than anything. This particular rich person could not change his priorities and did not follow Jesus. He was very sorrowful about his decision, but still he chose to cling to his earthly wealth. This young ruler had the opportunity to be taught by Jesus and could have been part of Jesus' disciples, teaching the Jews throughout Galilee and Judea. However, his earthly treasures were more important to him and he turned away from Jesus. How sad that this young man did not make the right decision.

However, Jesus did have rich followers. Joseph of Arimathea was rich and owned the private tomb where Jesus was buried after His death on the cross. This was where the women discovered Jesus had risen from the dead! His apostle, Matthew, was a tax collector and was rich. Zacchaeus was also a rich follower. After Zacchaeus began to follow Jesus, he gave half of his goods to the poor and restored fourfold anything he had taken falsely. In the Old Testament, we know Abraham, Lot, Job, David, and many others were rich. All of these rich followers put God first, not their personal wealth.

Let's go back to Jesus' Sermon on the Mount and the woe to the rich. Jesus warned the rich that it is easy to become very comfortable with ourselves and to forget our dependence on God. When you have a nice house and car, closets full of clothes, food, and money for vacations—well, you might forget that you need God. You don't long for heaven when every desire is fulfilled here on earth. This is what happened to the rich young ruler.

After the rich young ruler left sorrowfully, Jesus said that it was easier for a camel to go through the eye of a needle than to get to heaven. All the people who heard this asked, *"Who then can be saved?"* Jesus assured them with God, all things are possible. When rich people depend on God's grace, obey His will, and use their blessings for God's glory, they reach heaven. Our reward for our earthly sacrifices is *"in the age to come eternal life"* (Luke 18:30).

Reflections

You can be a rich Christian and go to heaven—it is just harder. It is harder because you often depend on yourself and not on God, or because you don't make God your priority. Don't be like the rich young ruler. Be like Jesus' followers who happened to be rich. The rich are told how to be pleasing to God in these verses of 1 Timothy 6:18-19, *"Let them do good, that they be rich in good works, ready to give, willing to share, storing up for themselves a good foundation for the time to come, that they may lay hold on eternal life."* People rich in spiritual wealth hold on to eternal life, making these good words to follow!

The Pursuit of Happiness

The second paragraph of the Declaration of Independence begins with these words: "We hold these truths to be self-evident, that all men are created equal, that they are endowed by their Creator with certain unalienable Rights, which among these are Life, Liberty and the pursuit of Happiness." The pursuit of happiness may be the only words of the Declaration that most Americans remember and a happy life is their primary goal.

Wikipedia defines happiness as a *"mental state of well-being characterized by positive or pleasant emotions ranging from contentment to intense joy."*[3] Webster's Dictionary defines happiness as "a state of well-being and contentment or a pleasurable or satisfying experience."[4] Happiness sounds like a good thing!

So let's see what the Bible says about happiness. In the New King James version, the words "happy" and "happiness" occur only 24 times in both the Old and New Testament! For comparison, the word "faith" occurs 252 times (only 9 times in Old Testament), the word "grace" occurs 145 times (only 18 times in Old Testament), and the word "hope" occurs 151 times (83 times in Old Testament). Wonder if faith, grace, and hope are more important than happiness?

Of those 24 utilizations of "happy" and "happiness," four are used in a political sense (Psa. 137:8, 9; Isa. 32:13; Jer. 12:1), e.g., "O daughter of Babylon, who are to be destroyed, Happy the one who repays you as you have served us!" Six utilizations are used relating to a sense of contentment (Gen. 30:13; Deut. 24:5; Pss. 127:5; 128:2; Prov. 14:21; Acts 26:2), e.g., "When you eat the labor of your hands, You shall be happy,

---

[3] http:en.wikipedia.org/wiki/Happiness. Wikipedia.org, N.D. 04/04/2012

[4] http://www.merriam-webster.com/dictionary/happiness. 04/05/2012

and it shall be well with you." All of the remaining utilizations (14) pertain to our relationship with God (Deut. 33:29; 1 Kings 10:8; 2 Chron. 9:7; Job 5:17; Pss. 34:1; 144:15; 146:1, 5; Prov. 3:13, 18; 16:20; 28:14; 29:18; Rom. 14:22), e.g., *"Happy are the people whose God is the LORD!"*

Clearly our relationship with God is a way to be happy, but is it God's goal for us to be happy while we live on earth? Unfortunately for all Declaration of Independence readers, the pursuit of happiness is not God's mission for us. God expects obedient faith from Christians and sometimes our obedience conflicts with our worldly goals which we think will make us happy.

This conflict may make our lives uncomfortable and we possibly might not be happy with our earthly lives. However, we should be happy—even joyful—with our spiritual life in God. In this type of situation, James wrote, *"My brethren, count it all joy when you fall into various trials, knowing that the testing of your faith produces patience"* (James 1:2-3). When our spiritual life has priority over our earthly life, then our happiness rests in God. These trials help us to grow and mature as Christians and to understand that heaven is our home. In this same chapter, James concludes, *"Blessed is the man who endures temptation; for when he has been approved, he will receive the crown of life which the Lord has promised to those who love Him"* (James 1:12).

Going back into the Old Testament, we find Solomon, the king of Israel, who was blessed by God with peace, wealth, and wisdom. Solomon knew a lot about the pursuit of happiness, but he found that his relationship with God was the most important. He wrote these two verses about pursuing earthly pleasures to make himself happy (Eccl. 2:10-11):

> Whatever my eyes desired I did not keep from them. I did not withhold my heart from any pleasure, for my heart rejoiced in all my labor; and this was my reward from all my labor. Then I looked on all the works that my hands had done and on the labor in which I had toiled; and indeed all was vanity and grasping for the wind. There was no profit under the sun.

Solomon found that the pursuit of happiness did not bring him into a mental state of well-being characterized by pleasant emotions, but his relationship with God did. Solomon summarized our rights as far as God is concerned in Ecclesiastes 12:13b: *"Fear God and keep His commandments, for this is the whole duty of man."*

Sometimes we think God will overlook our sin, because He wants us to be happy. However, Christians are not promised an easy life. In Hebrews 11, Paul tells us that early Biblical heroes were tortured, mocked, scourged, imprisoned, stoned, sawn in two, and slain with the sword. They wandered about in sheepskins and goatskins and were destitute, afflicted, and tormented. Even the Apostle Paul was beaten, shipwrecked, imprisoned, and finally killed. They did not ask God to make them happy, because their goal was to follow God's commandments and to make God happy.

Our happiness comes from a strong relationship with God. Sometimes we don't wear the latest high fashion, because it is not modest. Sometimes we don't sleep late on Sunday, because we worship God with the saints. Sometimes we don't make an advantageous business deal, because we don't lie, cheat, or steal. True happiness cannot be tied up with earthly measures. Solomon still has the best advice: *"He who heeds the word wisely will find good, and whoever trusts in the LORD, happy is he"* (Prov. 16:20).

Satan's Battle

People often talk about God battling Satan and say that Christ's resurrection was Satan's defeat. This idea implies God and Christ could be defeated by Satan. Christ's death was a sacrifice for our sin so we can be acceptable to God as a sinless person. God hates sin and we cannot be with God as sinners. Christ's death and resurrection removed our sins, so we can be acceptable to God. God predetermined this path for Christ and us before time began. Satan's battle is really with us as he tries to persuade us to follow him and not God. God cannot be defeated, but we can.

Our God is omnipotent and invincible. While Stephen is preaching to the Sanhedrin council, he quotes the prophet Isaiah (Acts 7:49): *"Heaven is My throne, And earth is My footstool."* God rules throughout His creation and the earth where we live is only a small footstool for Him. God does not battle Satan, because He is the Creator and is always greater than Satan and any part of His creation. The battle is ours and God supports us while we fight Satan for our souls. Isaiah knew this. Stephen knew this. Satan knows this.

Before time began, God planned Christ's sacrifice and resurrection so man could be sinless and receive the hope of heaven. The Apostle Peter taught this in the 1 Peter 1:19-21, *"...with the precious blood of Christ, ... He indeed was foreordained before the foundation of the world, but was manifest in these last times for you who through Him believe in God, who raised Him from the dead."* God loved us and planned a path for us to live sinlessly with Him in heaven. This is the purpose of Christ's death and resurrection. God's destruction of Satan is also not questionable as Satan will be *thrown into the lake of fire* at the end of time. Until then, Satan's goal is to destroy man whom God loves.

The book of 1 Peter encourages Christians facing battles with Satan. The book opens with the assurance that Christ's resurrection guarantees a heavenly reward: *"Blessed be the God and Father of our Lord Jesus Christ, who according to His abundant mercy has begotten us again to a living hope through the resurrection of Jesus Christ from the dead, to an inheritance incorruptible and undefiled and that does not fade away, reserved in heaven for you"* (1:3-4). Christ's resurrection guarantees our promise of eternal life in heaven. This is the same promise given to Abraham when God promised Abraham that through him all nations would be blessed. This blessing was Christ's resurrection which gives us the hope of heaven.

1 Peter warns us that Satan is our personal enemy. *"Be sober, be vigilant; because your adversary the devil walks about like a roaring lion, seeking whom he may devour"* (5:8). We must be thoughtful and watchful as we live our daily lives to give Satan no opening for attack. Satan enjoys the sport of drawing Christians away from God. In the book of Job, Satan taunted God and insisted that Job only followed God when following was easy. Of course, we know Job was faithful to God even when Satan attacked Job on every front. Satan could not devour Job, but he still seeks to devour us.

Satan uses his personal knowledge about us as his primary weapons. *"But each one is tempted when he is drawn away by his own desires and enticed. Then, when desire has conceived, it gives birth to sin"* (James 1:14-15a). Sometimes we are our own worst enemy in our battle with Satan and sin. Often the reason we sin is our blind desire for earthy treasure and our rejection of God's commandments. We want a nice house, job, and car so much that we ignore studying our Bible and fellowship with other Christians. Remember a person standing alone is easier for Satan to entice!

The next verse in 1 Peter is the battle plan for our ongoing war with Satan. *"Resist him, steadfast in the faith, knowing that the same sufferings are experienced by your brotherhood in the world"* (5:9). Daily we must fight against the Satan and cannot ignore his influence in the smallest details of our life. However, we also know when we fight against Satan, he flees from us (James 4:7)! *"Therefore submit to God.*

Resist the devil and he will flee from you." Satan is a strong adversary, but we can defeat him.

As we battle Satan, it is important to know we are not alone. In 1 Peter 5:7, Christians are told to cast their worries on God as He cares for them. Then, in the very next verse, they are warned to be watchful and resist Satan who is their adversary! Peter knew Christians needed God in their battles with Satan, who is like a roaring lion seeking people to lead away from God. So Peter reminded them of God's concern for them first, following with that reminder of Satan's ravenous appetite. We need God against such a powerful predator and God wants us to depend on Him, because He loves us and wants us to win over Satan. Both of these verses are important to remember – the first is our pledge from God that He is with us and the second as a warning about Satan's determination.

In Matthew 28:20, the apostles are assured, *"I am with you always, even to the end of the age."* This promise is a guarantee to all of us when Satan is pressing us hard on all sides. The strength and comfort we gain from knowing God is with us until the end of time is necessary in our daily battles. Every Christian must remember the Creator of everything is with each of us to the end of time. He stands with us and carries us during our struggles and hardest conflicts. What wonderful reassurance in our ongoing battles with Satan!

Satan may be a powerful enemy, but when the omnipotent and invincible God is our partner, Satan can never prevail!

The Pleasure of Anticipation

Anticipation is one of the most underrated pleasures of life. Remember the anticipation of opening presents when you were a child? It seemed like the day for opening the presents would never come. Then the magical day was there and all those presents were for you! Remember the anticipation of a vacation? We think of all the things we are going to do, the people we are going to see, the food we are going to eat, and places we are going to go. Vacations are fun and the anticipation of a vacation is almost as good as the vacation itself.

Anticipation can be sweet and very exciting, but some anticipated events are not quickly obtained. We anticipate our graduation dates from school, our marriages, the birth of our children, careers, and retirement. As we anticipate these milestones, we work steadily toward those goals. This type of anticipation requires planning and effort on our part. The pleasure of these anticipations is not evident each day, but it still sustains us as we labor toward our goals. For example, Jacob worked seven years for Rachel, but they seemed like a few days due to his love for her.

Our greatest anticipation is heaven and our rest with God after our life on earth is finished. Heaven may seem as far away to us as those presents did when we were children. However, our time on earth speeds away as fast as our childhood did! This wonderful present is our inheritance promised to us by God and He has given us plenty of clues about it already! Our inheritance is *"incorruptible and undefiled and does not fade away, reserved in heaven for you, who are kept by the power of God through faith for salvation ready to be revealed in the last time"* (1 Pet. 1:4-5).

Do we sometimes get tired while we are waiting for heaven? Even children stress and cry before the time for presents. The work, strain, and anxiety that come before all good things take a toll on us. Remember how hard we worked to get ready for our vacation? We had hotel reservations to make, transportation to arrange, family members to coordinate, clothes to wash and pack, and all of those other preparations that make us so exhausted. Sometimes we wonder if all the work is worth the vacation!

Christians can face hard times and hard labor while anticipating heaven. Sometimes the work to get ready for heaven includes illness, financial hardship, family catastrophes, and many burdensome challenges to our faith. We become so tired that we forget what we are working toward and our anticipation is not enough to sustain us.

We know the first century Christians faced persecutions including torture and death. Their anticipation of heaven had to be substantial to maintain their faith during those hard times. Our anticipation of heaven can build on their example of faithfulness and their ability to find joy in trials. The first century Christians knew their ordeals made the anticipation of heaven sweeter and the reality of heaven more certain. The Apostle Peter encouraged them in his letter to those believers facing persecution and suffering:

> In this you greatly rejoice, though now for a little while, if need be, you have been grieved by various trials, that the genuineness of your faith, being much more precious than gold that perishes, though it is tested by fire, may be found to praise, honor, and glory at the revelation of Jesus Christ, whom having not seen you love. Though now you do not see Him, yet believing, you rejoice with joy inexpressible and full of glory, receiving the end of your faith—the salvation of your souls (1 Pet. 1:6-9).

One of my favorite verses encapsulating the anticipation of heaven and the strain of reaching for this prize was written by the Apostle Paul while he was facing the possibility of capital punishment in a Roman prison. Paul never doubted God and even preached to his Praetorian guards! "Brethren, I do not count myself to have apprehended; but one thing I do, forgetting those things which are behind and reaching forward to those things which are ahead, I press toward the goal for the prize of the upward call of God in Christ Jesus" (Phil. 3:13-14).

Paul did not let the stress of captivity weigh down his anticipation of heaven. He found joy in his present circumstances; so much, in fact, that members of Caesar's household became Christians. He was looking forward to his inheritance—God's promise of heaven and salvation of his soul.

The flip side of Paul's anticipation of heaven is the nonbelievers' dread. In Hebrews 10:26-31, nonbelievers are warned about the judgment of God. *"For if we sin willfully after we have received the knowledge of the truth, there no longer remains a sacrifice for sins, but a certain fearful expectation of judgment, and fiery indignation which will devour the adversaries. Anyone who has rejected Moses' law dies without mercy on the testimony of two or three witnesses. Of how much worse punishment, do you suppose, will he be thought worthy who has trampled the Son of God underfoot, counted the blood of the covenant by which he was sanctified a common thing, and insulted the Spirit of grace? For we know Him who said, 'Vengeance is Mine, I will repay,' says the Lord. And again, 'The Lord will judge His people.' It is a fearful thing to fall into the hands of the living God."* The judgment of the living God is definitely more to dread than a dentist drill!

Our anticipation of heaven is a sweet expectation and better than presents and vacations! God's promises and our faith support us as we anticipate and work toward this goal. We reach forward even when the work is hard and find joy in our anticipation of heaven. Yes, anticipation is an underrated pleasure of life!

Am I Like My Father?

My older son was at work and noticed he was wringing his hands as his father does when thinking. He let his thoughts wander to remember other ways he was like his father. He remembered things he said, things he did, and things he thought which were like his father's words, deeds, and beliefs. He also noticed some of these words, deeds, and beliefs he consciously decided to emulate and sometimes he copied his father unconsciously. He was glad to have a strong earthly father to imitate and realized he needed to imitate his heavenly Father, too.

Earthly fathers teach their children how to love, live, work, and enjoy life. A good father takes care of his children, prepares them to be strong adults that love God, and are an example for their children in everything they do. Their children see how their fathers work on their jobs, treat their families and community, and honor God. A father's lessons are not just how to tie a hook on a fishing line, but how to live.

A country song by Rodney Atkins has these lines "I've been watching you, dad ain't that cool? I'm your buckaroo, I want to be like you. . . . I want to do everything you do. So I've been watching you."[5] In this song, the little boy had learned a few bad words from his dad, which was not a good thing, and the dad was sad about his example. Contrast this with the ending of the song where the little boy had learned from his dad to pray to God as a friend. Now this was something great and the dad was proud to be that example!

The dad didn't know he was teaching his son in his daily living, but the little boy was learning to be like his dad. Fortunately this dad learned to be a better man himself from his son! This little boy was

---

[5] "Watching You," Rodney Atkins, *You're Going Through Hell*, 2006.

consciously copying his dad when he was praying. I wish all children had this lesson.

Sometimes we unconsciously imitate our fathers. Our attitudes toward faith, family, school, sports, and work are often learned from our fathers when we are young—not even knowing we were getting a lesson. As we mature, we must evaluate our attitudes to ensure they are as God intended. Good earthy fathers foster outlooks with compassion, love, effort, and devotion to God. When we are taught in this manner, then imitation of our earthly fathers helps us to be more like our heavenly Father. When we are not fortunate enough to have a wonderful earthly father to imitate, then we must consciously imitate our heavenly Father to be a good person and a strong Christian.

Our heavenly Father cares and is compassionate to all of us. He dresses the lilies in the field and takes care of us. We begin by consciously imitating Him and soon adopt His characteristics unconsciously when God's ways become our ways. As we let God fill our lives, we adopt His attitudes and practices until we find ourselves like Him. We are the little boy in the country song—watching our Father and acting like Him.

Jesus worked hard to be like His Father. In John 5:19-20, Jesus told the Jews, *"Most assuredly, I say to you, the Son can do nothing of Himself, but what He sees the Father do; for whatever He does, the Son also does in like manner. For the Father loves the Son, and shows Him all things that He Himself does; and He will show Him greater works than these, that you may marvel."* Jesus, the Son, did what the Father did because the Father loved the Son. If Jesus strove to do what our heavenly Father did, then how can we do less?

Our heavenly Father loves us. As we emulate Him in our lives, our conscious imitations become our unconscious habits. We become more faithful to God, hopeful of our salvation, and gracious to others. As our character is strengthened and matures, we are becoming more like our heavenly Father and that is a "cool" thing.

Two Men Named Ananias

There are two men named Ananias with two very different stories in the New Testament. The first Ananias lied to God. The second Ananias taught a dangerous man about the gospel. Both men "believed," but the men did not do the same thing with their belief.

The story of the first Ananias is found in Acts 5. This story happened in the early days of the church. Many Jews had come to Jerusalem for Pentecost and had been baptized after hearing the gospel message. These new Christians lingered in Jerusalem to learn more and after a time, many had spent all the money they had brought with them. Many local Christians sold their belongings to provide food and shelter for their fellow Christians and bought the proceeds of these sales to the apostles for distribution to the needy Christians. This is where the story of the first Ananias begins. This Ananias and his wife, Sapphira, sold some land, too. Ananias and Sapphira had decided to keep part of the money for themselves, which was their rightful choice. However, when Ananias gave the money to the apostles, he claimed the amount was the full value of the land, for he wanted to be an important man in the Christian community. Peter told him, *"Why have you conceived this thing in your heart? You have not lied to men but to God."* Well, this Ananias fell dead right on the spot, which proved it was not a good thing to lie to God!

The story of the second Ananias is found in Acts 9. This Ananias was a regular person, like you or me, who had exemplary faith and was ready for God to use him. Of course, God needed this Ananias to perform a scary task. Jesus appeared to this Ananias in a vision and said to Ananias, *"Arise and go to the street called Straight, and inquire at the house of Judas for one called Saul of Tarsus, for behold, he is praying. And in a vision he has seen a man named Ananias coming in and putting his hand on him, so that he might receive his sight"* (Acts 9:11-12). Now this is a *hard* command for Ananias to obey. Any Christian who had left the Jewish faith was afraid of Saul, because Saul hunted them down and led them away in chains! Saul was a fervent persecutor of Jewish Christians and responsible for the death of many of them. However, Ananias overcame his fear of certain death and went as commanded to find Saul. He did what Jesus told him in the vision and found the blinded Saul. Ananias healed Saul's eyes, taught, and baptized him that night and was an integral part of the conversion of Saul who is better known to us as the Apostle Paul!

These two stories about men named Ananias have very different conclusions. The second Ananias believed in God and obeyed the will of God. He obeyed even when he was sure obedience would kill him and was instrumental in the conversion of Saul. The first Ananias believed in God, but lied about his contribution in order to be more important in the eyes of the Christian community. To this Ananias, the admiration of other men was more important than being truthful to God. Isn't it a funny thing that belief in God wasn't enough to save the first Ananias? He was struck dead there in front of the apostles and all the men he wanted to impress.

So what can we learn about two men named Ananias? Real faith in God is not just belief in God. Real faith requires action and obedience to God's commandments. All of us must be like the second Ananias by demonstrating our faith with our actions, and not like the first Ananias seeking glory from men!

Hypocrisy in Christians

Recently one of my cousins posted a Facebook status talking about hypocrisy in Christians. She works in the food service industry and frequently waited on "Christian" groups. These rude groups considered themselves to be more righteous than the serving staff who were working on Sunday. This is definitely not how Christians should ever be and not the attitude Jesus taught! Jesus continually taught us to be humble, kind, and generous. He never taught anyone was better or worth more than another person and would not approve of "Christians" being rude during Sunday lunch.

In the Sermon on the Mount, Jesus frequently spoke of hypocrisy. For example, Jesus condemned doing good deeds to look good to other men or acting like you are more religious than others. The following verses from the Sermon on the Mount (Matthew 6) directly show how Jesus viewed hypocritical attitudes. Hypocrites are interested in looking superior to others, but this does not make them any better!

> Take heed that you do not do your charitable deeds before men, to be seen by them. Otherwise you have no reward from your Father in heaven. Therefore, when you do a charitable deed, do not sound a trumpet before you as the hypocrites do in the synagogues and in the streets, that they may have glory from men. Assuredly, I say to you, they have their reward. But when you do a charitable deed, do not let your left hand know what your right hand is doing, that your charitable deed may be in secret; and your Father who sees in secret will Himself reward you openly (6:1-4).

> And when you pray, you shall not be like the hypocrites. For they love to pray standing in the synagogues and on the corners of the streets, that they may be seen by men. Assuredly, I say to you, they have their reward. But you, when you pray, go into your room, and when you have shut your

door, pray to your Father who is in the secret place; and your Father who sees in secret will reward you openly (6:5-6).

Moreover when you fast, do not be like the hypocrites with a sad countenance. For they disfigure their faces that they may appear to men to be fasting. Assuredly, I say to you, they have their reward (6:16).

Notice in the first set of verses, Jesus did not say that *if* you do charitable deeds, but *when* you do charitable deeds. He expected everyone to do good things for other people for the glory of God as generosity is part of a Christian's daily life. A hypocrite is boastful and blows his own horn anytime he does a good deed. Again, a true Christian is humble and kind, not performing good deeds for personal accolades.

In all of these verses, Jesus did not want us to be righteous in appearance only, so that our goodness is for the praise of men. Hypocrites are not fooling God! He is looking for real righteousness which comes from your heart with the goal of worship and praise to God. A small, sincere deed is worth everything, but a huge, boastful deed is worth nothing. God values our true purpose for the deed and men value only the deed.

One of the best known verses from the Sermon on the Mount is often called the Golden Rule. *"Therefore, whatever you want men to do to you, do also to them"* (Matt. 7:12). This was a dramatic change to the Jews of that day. Their attitude was to do no harm. Jesus taught to do good to others, a more active attitude of good will to our fellowman. Christians must actively seek ways to treat others in the manner that they want to be treated themselves. Rudeness cannot live under this rule!

During Jesus' life on earth, the Pharisees were very similar to the "Christians" in my cousin's Facebook post. The Pharisees were a Jewish sect which followed strict religious regulations and were certain they were the most righteous of all Jews. They were proud of their class distinction and more proud they weren't "regular" Jews. Jesus routinely condemned hypocrisy and the Pharisees would top His hypocrite list. Instead of being praised for their goodness, Jesus used them as examples of bad behavior in parables. The parable of the Pharisee and tax collector (Luke 18:9-14) showed a Pharisee as the hypocrite and the sinful tax collector as the more righteous man. In this parable, the Pharisee prayed on the street corner for all to see and the tax collector prayed humbly. In this very public place, the Pharisee commended himself for all his good deeds and thanked God for making him a Pharisee! In the private corner, the tax collector humbly asked God to forgive his sins. Even though the Pharisee thought he was more righteous than the sinful tax collector, Jesus did not think so!

We need to act like humble Christians every day! We are not acting as Jesus taught us if we are rude and pompous to others. Our negative example may turn them away from Jesus, which would be a dreadful result of our actions. When you act like my cousin's "Christians," you have not learned from Jesus' Sermon on the Mount.

Having It God's Way

Our western lifestyle encourages us to live self-centered lives with rugged individualism. Living a comfortable and self-fulfilled life is our priority and a national goal. We even expect fast food to be "our way" as we custom order our hamburgers with only our favorite toppings. Our independence is applauded and encouraged in every classroom and all media! How can there be room for God when having it our own way is the main concern of our lives? Is God happy with that?

Christians want personal fulfillment at church and may expect worship to fill their spiritual need. We might worship God in ways to meet our personal preferences and spiritual needs and change things around to make us happy as we worship. When we are happy and fulfilled, then surely God is smiling too. After all, happy people work harder and longer and God would approve of that!

Unfortunately, worshipping to please ourselves is not the best idea. We need to accept that God has told us how He wants to be worshipped and making us happy is not His goal. When Paul asked God to make him happy by removing the thorn in Paul's flesh, the purpose in His response was not to make Paul happy. In 2 Corinthians 12:9, Paul tells us of God's response, *"My grace is sufficient for you, for My strength is made perfect in weakness."* Paul gladly accepted this, so the power of Christ could be with him. Paul knew it is more important to learn to be happy with whatever makes God happy. A wonderful thing about making God happy is He has told us how to do it. The ancillary point to knowing God's instruction is that when those instructions are not followed, God is not happy!

In Numbers 20:7-12, God had told Moses to speak to the rock to bring water to the thirsty Israelites. The Israelites' constant whining and complaining had made Moses angry and they were on his last nerve. His frustration was clearly evident when he struck the rock and said, *"Hear now, you rebels! Must we bring water for you out of this rock?"* (20:10). Now the Israelites were happy for they had water and Moses was happy for the Israelites were not whining. However, God was not happy! Moses had not followed His instructions nor given God the credit for providing the water. For punishment, God did not allow Moses to enter the Promised Land.

2 Samuel 6:1-9 is the story of David moving the ark to Jerusalem from the house of Abinadab. For expediency, David had loaded the ark on an ox cart and had Abinadab's sons, Uzzah and Ahio, drive the cart. David and all the people were celebrating as they accompanied the ark to Jerusalem. During the journey, the oxen stumbled and Uzzah held the ark so it wouldn't fall off the cart. For his concern about the ark, God struck Uzzah dead right there! Why would God strike a man dead for taking care of holy items? The problems were no one was supposed to touch the ark and it wasn't to be transported on an ox cart! David was afraid of God that day!

Leviticus 9 describes offerings made to God by Aaron, the priests, and the people. They offered bulls, rams, calves, and goats as a wave offerings, a sin offering, a burnt offering, and peace offerings. God was pleased with these offerings and *"the glory of the LORD appeared to all the people"* (9:23). A fire went out from the LORD and consumed the burnt offering. Oh, what a glorious occasion! Everyone was so excited, because God was clearly pleased with them. The next chapter continues the story. *"Then Nadab and Abihu, the sons of Aaron, each took his censer and put fire in it, put incense on it, and offered profane fire before the Lord, which He had not commanded them"* (10:1-2). A fire went out again from the LORD and devoured Nadab and Abihu! Why would God do that when Nadab and Abihu were trying to offer Him the aroma of the incense? Clearly improving worship had not made God happy. Nadab and Abihu wanted to continue with the enthusiasm of the moment and improved God's worship service. However, their profane fire was not wanted by God and their improved worship cost them their lives!

What do these examples tell us? God wants our worship and our worship makes Him happy when it follows His instructions. God wants what He wants and His goal is not to please us. As we are living our lives and having it our way, we must be sure our worship is God's way.

In Colossians 1:10, Paul prays for the Colossians to have a walk worthy of the Lord and to be fully pleasing to Him. Our worship must be pleasing to God—what a concept! Worship pleasing to God is our goal, not worshipping to make ourselves happy. We and the Colossians have the same objective during our worship—to have it God's way.

Wishes and Hopes

Let's talk about our wishes and hopes. However, the first thing to do before talking about wishes and hopes is to understand the difference between a wish and a hope. We often use both words to mean the same thing in our daily conversations. We might say, "I hope it rains" and "I wish it would rain" without thinking of the distinction in the sentence meanings.

Let's go to our trusty dictionaries to see the differentiation of these two words. In many dictionaries, a "wish" is defined as an expressed will or desire and "hope" is defined as expectation of fulfillment or success. So the real difference between "wish" and "hope" is that hope has the earnest expectation of success compared to a stated desire for wish.

So hoping for rain on a cloudless day with no storm fronts on the horizon is really a wish. There is no evidence of any chance for rain and our hope for rain is really a desire or wish for rain without any real expectation of drops falling out of the sky.

Hoping for rain when thunder is rolling and lightning is on the horizon is an earnest expectation of a storm with rain and not just a wish. In this instance, there is evidence of rain in the thunder and lightning and so this hope for rain has evidence for success.

What does a Christian wish for? We wish for health for ourselves and our families. We wish for happiness, prosperity, world peace, and understanding among all people. We wish for delightful picnics at the river, good times at the zoo, and fun at our friend's house. Nothing is wrong with any of these wishes. These are things we want to happen. Sometimes we can do something to help our wishes, sometimes we cannot.

Often we don't even remember our wishes. They are wistful or lightly considered, because they are not important or meaningful. We wish for our team to hit a home run in their last bat in the last inning. However, that wish is not remembered after the game is over– no matter if our team won or lost.

What does a Christian hope for? We hope for eternal life and glory of heaven with God. We have this earnest expectation due to our knowledge of the gospel, faith in God, and the resurrection of Christ. We know the gospel message is given to us in our Bibles and *"whatever things were written . . . for our learning, so we through the patience and comfort of the Scriptures might have hope"* (Rom. 15:4). Our learning and knowledge of the gospel are the basis of our hope, our sincere expectation for success of eternal life and glory of heaven with God. Without knowing the gospel, we cannot have any such hope and have no basis for our faith in God providing us eternal life in heaven.

The lynchpin for our hope is our faith in the resurrection of Christ. *"Blessed be the God and Father of our Lord Jesus Christ, who according to His abundant mercy has begotten us again to a living hope through the resurrection of Jesus Christ from the dead, to an inheritance incorruptible and undefiled and that does not fade away, reserved in heaven for you"* (1 Pet. 1:3-4). The whole gospel is based on our living hope which is Christ, because Christ lives! Our world was made by God through Christ who came to earth to die and live again. Our certainty that Christ lives even though He was crucified is the reason for our hope. We know we can achieve our hope of eternal life in heaven which is the success required for our hope.

However, how can we know Christ is alive when we have not seen Him? How can our faith be based on this hope? *"Faith is the substance of things hoped for, the evidence of things not seen. . . .By faith we understand that the worlds were framed by the word of God, so that the things which are seen were not made of things which are visible"* (Heb. 11:1, 3). Our faith is strong because we know it is impossible for God to lie, which anchors our hope (Heb. 6:18-19). Not only do we have our faith in God, but all the evidences of God which we can see concretely prove God is our Creator. We have the beautiful stars at night, the mountain vistas, the canyon grandeur, the synergy of all plant and animal life—

we have our whole world! Our faith is a living hope in a living Christ, because God's evidences are everywhere. These evidences are part of what makes our hope a certainty and not a wish.

Our hope in God brings us comfort and strength in our daily life, because it is an earnest expectation and not a simple desire. Of course, if we don't desire or wish for heaven, then we certainly will never have success in obtaining it. We must have a desire of heaven to have the hope of heaven; without this desire, then the work to obtain the necessary knowledge of the gospel will never happen. This is another difference in hope and a wish. We must remember our hope each day– all day. Hope is not a wistful thought flying through our mind, but is thoughtful and certain. It lives in our mind as a foundation for our actions and plans and becomes part of whom and what we are. Christian hope is the best thing for any Christian to have in all situations.

The best ending for this article is to use one of Paul's salutations. *"Now may the God of hope fill you with all joy and peace in believing, that you may abound in hope by the power of the Holy Spirit"* (Rom. 15:13). Hope grounded in God is certain expectation and most certainly is much more than a wish!

Beacons on the Hill

Just think about the influences of the people in your life. I am not only talking about close friends, but the people you see every day and people who see you. Young and old can be encouraging or draining without realizing their effect on those around them. One person can make you smile just by walking toward you and another can steal the sun from the sky to darken your whole day. What type of influence do you have on others? Does a Christian light shine from your life into an associate's life providing strength and cheer? Or does angst spill over from your cup into theirs?

Sometimes we don't know what result our everyday actions have on other people. We don't think anyone is paying attention or we aren't important enough in other people's lives to make a difference. This is so untrue!

The tap-tap of the older man's cane as he walks to his seat for every worship service encourages everyone else there. Some days he feels good. Some days he feels bad. Still he is there, worshipping and praising God. He doesn't know anyone is looking, but everyone is! The other seniors in their seats see him. The empty nesters making new lives see him. The young parents struggling with babies see him. The teenagers chatting together see him. The preschoolers playing in the aisles see him. Everyone sees him and he encourages faithfulness in all of them. He doesn't know the influence he has on these people just by being there and living his faithful life.

A young person can be as inspirational as an older person. Imagine a twenty-something showing up unannounced to babysit two preschoolers for a lady pregnant with her third child. Imagine a high-schooler posting Bible verses on FaceBook for daily encouragement to her "friends." Imagine college students and young married couples who are faithful when our culture emphasizes everything else. Imagine a young person "adopting" someone needing special attention and moral support. All of these young people act like Christian lights because they are beacons on the hill and their light floods into others' lives!

Actions do not have to be big to have a positive influence. The widow in the temple observed by Jesus giving her two mites (small copper coins worth a penny) into the treasury was not performing a grand deed (Mark 12:41-43). However, Jesus valued her contribution more than all the riches given by others. This widow could not give much and did not have anything else to offer; however, she was doing everything she could and living her faith. She was like the old man with the cane who is living his faith. This widow has influence in our lives today and she didn't know we were watching!

The Philippian Christians did not know we were watching when they contributed to Paul's ministry. However, we are still learning from their supportive attitude, hospitality, and generosity. For example, Lydia met Paul on the riverbank where he preached the gospel to her and her household. After she was baptized, she hosted him and his fellow travelers in her home during their time there (Acts 16:15). The Philippians sent money to Paul for his expenses several times (Phil. 4:15-16). The people of that church did not give their money to be put on a public list for honor. They were contributing to the gospel in a manner available to them. Small actions develop into big actions which have lasting influence.

Mothers and fathers are examples of unnoticed beacons. Lois and Eunice were the grandmother and mother of Timothy who became one of our great early evangelists (2 Tim. 1:5). How could they know we were watching when they taught baby Timothy gospel songs and helped him to learn gospel verses? How could they know we were watching when they taught young Timothy to stand up for truth and encouraged him to preach? Mothers and fathers are probably the most watched individuals ever! Their actions teach their young ones how to live, think, and interact, especially when no one is watching.

I cannot stress how small actions can have a huge wave of influence. When a visitor is not greeted by the Christian brethren, why would he want to learn more about the gospel? A cold shoulder during worship is chilling to fledging interest. Why would a newcomer expect a warm welcome after continuing to study the gospel and being baptized, when no one is interested in the beginning? Our children watch us at worship and learn from us. They learn how adults revere and love God. If the sermon or the Sunday school lesson is not important to the parents, why would they be important to the children? Don't think no one is watching. In these examples, both the visitor and our young ones are watching.

How about our actions when we are not at worship. It is imperative for our Christian light to shine everywhere, not just at church. For example, our influence at a store depends on our actions there. A pleasant man making suggestions or reasonable requests reflects a Christian attitude with positive influence, while a rude man with loud complaints does not demonstrate a Christian spirit and has destructive influence. People really notice what others are doing. For example, a lady asked my son if he went to church while he was clerking at a pet food store. She said he had a Christian attitude toward work by always smiling and working hard. Who knew someone was watching while he was making extra money for college?

Do you reach out to help others during their hard times? This is easy, exciting, and satisfying when the need is special like disastrous tornadoes or Katrina. Then everyone pitches in with organized relief drives and anyone not involved feels left out. What about those quiet people? The lady with a sick husband, a family with a handicapped child, the lonely widow, the chronically sick neighbor – what about them? Small actions make tidal waves here! A card, a visit, a service! These actions aren't huge to you, but make a Christian beacon of light shine on them. Probably our best actions are those we perform when we think no one is looking.

We don't have to be old or young or in the middle to have an influence in someone else's life. Our influence starts with our actions. Christian actions have such a wonderful influence everywhere we go and we never know who is watching!

Are You a Problem-Solver?

Are you the go-to person for problem-solving—the person that fixes things for other people in hard circumstances? Often problem-solving is proof of our resilience, knowledge, control, and positive evidence of our abilities, especially in stressful situations. Research suggests that people who are able to come up with solutions are better able to cope with problems than those who cannot.[6]

Problem-solving includes identifying the problem, forming a strategy to solve the problem, and then implementing the problem-solving strategy. Really sounds simple, doesn't it? But the fact is that a lot of life's problems cannot be solved by us. Where do you go with an unsolvable problem when you are a problem solver? How can you depend on others to fix your problem when you know there is no solution? The truth is problem-solvers need God.

The nobleman in John 4 is an example of a Biblical problem-solver with faith in God. This nobleman was a royal officer in service of Herod Antipas and certainly a man used to solving big problems and having many people depend on his knowledge and abilities. The nobleman's son was sick and at the point of death. The nobleman had done everything he could to make his son well, but his son was still dying. The nobleman could not fix this problem!

The nobleman heard Jesus had come into Galilee and went to Jesus, pleading for Jesus to come heal his son. The nobleman knew he needed help to save his son's life and believed Jesus could do just that. Because of his faith, Jesus told the nobleman to go back home and that his son would live. The nobleman's servants confirmed the boy

---

[6] "10 Ways to Become More Resilient." http://psychology.about.com/od/crisis-counseling/tp/become-more-resilient.htm. psychology.about.com, n.d. Web. 31 Dec 2011.

became well at the same hour in which Jesus told him the boy lived. The nobleman had faith in Jesus and depended on Him to heal his son which the problem-solving nobleman could not do himself.

This was good news for the nobleman, but what about our problems today? How can we depend on God to help us with our problems? Let's look in the book of Psalms to see how David depended on God with his problems. Remember, David spent years hiding in the desert from King Saul. Later when he was king, he waged many wars against enemies and then had conflicts within Israel. Often things would look desperate for David. In Psalm 7:1-2, David lamented, *"O LORD my God, in You I put my trust; Save me from all those who persecute me; And deliver me, Lest they tear me like a lion, Rending me in pieces, while there is none to deliver."* In this same psalm, David sang of his faith in God: *"My defense is of God, Who saves the upright in heart. God is a just judge, and God is angry with the wicked every day"* (7:10-11).

David used his faith in God as the primary approach in his problem-solving. David asked God what to do after learning of Saul's death (2 Sam. 2:1). David asked God whether he should battle the Philistines (2 Sam. 5:19). David worshipped God after the death of his and Bathsheba's son (2 Sam. 12:20). David rejoiced with God in good times, such as when the Ark of the Covenant was moved into the City of David (2 Sam. 6:14). Disaster occurred whenever David left God out of the problem-solving, such as when he didn't control his lust for Bathsheba. In this instance, leaving God out of the problem-solving resulted in an unintended pregnancy and the murder of Uriah the Hittite (2 Sam. 11).

We are more successful when we include God in our problem-solving instead of being a stand-alone problem-solver. Our anthem should be this song from David (2 Sam. 22:2-4): *"The LORD is my rock and my fortress and my deliverer; The God of my strength, in whom I will trust; My shield and the horn of my salvation, My stronghold and my refuge; My Savior . . . I will call upon the LORD, who is worthy to be praised."*

The best conclusion for a problem-solver is to start with Paul's statement in Romans 8. *"If God is for us, who can be against us?"* (Rom. 8:31). Including God in your problem-solving is the best start and the best finish!

Your Shame and God's Forgiveness

I know many Christians are ashamed of themselves and I am one myself. We are ashamed of our past deeds and lifestyles. We know God has forgiven our sins, but we cannot forgive ourselves. In our quiet thoughts, we wonder how God can forgive the bad things we have done when He hates sin so much.

In Romans 6:21, the Apostle Paul asks Christians about their shame of past deeds: *"What fruit did you have then in the things of which you are now ashamed? For the end of those things is death."* Many of those early Christians had engaged in very sinful activities which were common practices in their cultures. For example, both temple worship ceremonies and trade guild meetings often ended in drunkenness and immorality. These Christians had participated and probably enjoyed disgraceful activities centered on idol worship and related temple practices. They had many shameful sins weighing on their heart when they became Christians.

Many of us are ashamed of sins committed even when we knew of God and His law. We don't have the excuse of those early Roman Christians. We knew better! I am sure Peter put himself in this category. Peter had succumbed to the pressure during Jesus' trial and denied Jesus three times. Afterwards, he was so sorrowful and repented of this grave sin. Peter's shame in denying Jesus was intense, but he used his shame to be a firebrand gospel preacher in the early church.

It is also possible to do what you may think is right and be *very* wrong. A striking example is Paul. Paul knew the Old Law and not the gospel message. His sin was his zeal and delight in pursuing the destruction of the early church. Paul wrote to Timothy: *". . . Christ Jesus came into the world to save sinners, of whom I am chief"* (1 Tim. 1:15). Paul was so ashamed of the dreadful things he had done to persecute Christians, but he knew Jesus came to save sinners and had forgiven his sins.

Some of us are like the Christians in the Ephesian church. We used to be a zealous Christians, but have become lazy or now pursue other interests! Revelation 2:4-5 says this to the Ephesians: *"Nevertheless I have this against you, that you have left your first love. Remember therefore from where you have fallen; repent and do the first works, or else I will come to you quickly and remove your lampstand from its place—unless you repent."* The Ephesians had let their zeal for God and His grace become cold. They were busy doing all sorts of good things for the wrong reasons, but God was not their first love anymore. Their love of God and desire for grace was a distant thing to be picked up and dusted off at convenient times. We can be like this, too. Busy Christians whose deeds are not God-centered have left their first love like the Ephesian church did.

One of the clearest assurances of God's forgiveness is found in Hebrews 10:16-17, 22-23. *"This is the covenant that I will make with them after those days, says the Lord: I will put My laws into their hearts, and in their minds I will write them,"* then He adds, *"Their sins and their lawless deeds I will remember no more." . . . let us draw near with a true heart in full assurance of faith, having our hearts sprinkled from an evil conscience and our bodies washed with pure water. Let us hold fast the confession of our hope without wavering, for He who promised is faithful."*

God's forgiveness is assured to us! Our problem is forgiving ourselves! We will never forget the things we have done and shouldn't want to do that. We must use our personal history to be better, godlier people producing holy fruit, not evil deeds. Looking again at Romans 6:22-23, Paul writes, *"But now having been set free from sin, and having become slaves of God, you have your fruit to holiness, and the end, everlasting life. For the wages of sin is death, but the gift of God is eternal life in Christ Jesus our Lord."*

I know this is easy to say, but use your shame as fuel to produce good fruit. Make this negative a positive force for your work in God's kingdom and your goal to live a God-centered life. We cannot rewrite our personal histories, but must remember He forgives those who truly repent. God has forgiven us, no matter how embarrassing or bad our lives might have been. He wants us to be slaves to His righteousness producing righteous fruit.

Use your shame as a goad to be more like God each day. No, we won't be perfect. But with practice, we will be better Christians and our fruits will be sweeter. The Roman Christians were ashamed, but were strong Christians. Paul gave the Roman Christians this advice. *"For I am not ashamed of the gospel of Christ, for it is the power of God to salvation for everyone who believes"* (Rom. 1:16). Be like our ancient Roman brethren as slaves of God producing holy fruit leading to everlasting life. Use the shame of your sins to be the best Christian you can be and don't ever be ashamed of being a Christian!

Marco Polo

Imagine a hot summer day with children playing in a backyard pool. One of the children says, "Let's play Marco Polo and I will be it." Immediately there is laughing and splashing in the pool as all the other children scramble away. The first child closes his eyes while saying "Marco." All the other children respond "Polo" and try not to giggle. The first child with closed eyes listens for calls of "Polo" and tries to tag one of those giggling children. Of course, all the children are hiding in the pool and trying not to be found by the child calling "Marco."

Marco Polo is an innocent child's game. However, do we play Marco Polo with God? Are we hiding when God is calling for us? Hiding from God is not an innocent child's game.

Adam and Eve hid from God in the Garden of Eden after disobeying Him (Genesis 3:8-9). God was walking in the garden and calling for them to enjoy the cool of the evening with Him. Wouldn't it have been wonderful to have an intimate relationship with God and take evening walks with Him? But instead of looking forward to time with God, Adam and Eve hid from God and ignored His calls for them. They had done a shameful thing, disobeyed God, and were fearfully hiding from God due to their sin.

We can hide from God, because we fear He will learn of our sin. However, God already knew of Adam and Eve's sin and knows our sin, too. *"For His eyes are on the ways of man, and He sees all his steps. There is no darkness nor shadow of death where the workers of iniquity may hide themselves"* (Job. 34:21-22). God knows each sinful person and all his hiding places. The wonderful thing about God is He calls for us to come out of our hiding places all the time, but not as a game. God calls us, not to play hide and seek, but to repent of our sins and follow Him.

Our God is an omnipotent God and our almighty Creator. However, we don't have to be afraid of Him when we come to His call and obey His commands. In 1 Peter 1:15-19, we know God is fair: *"but as He who called you is holy, you also be holy in all your conduct, because it is written, 'Be holy, for I am holy.' And if you call on the Father, who without partiality judges according to each one's work, conduct yourselves throughout the time of your stay here in fear; knowing that you were not redeemed with corruptible things, like silver or gold, from your aimless conduct received by tradition from your fathers, but with the precious blood of Christ, as of a lamb without blemish and without spot."* Our fear is that we are not holy, so we hide ourselves from Him.

Another reason we hide from God is we don't want to do what God asks. Jonah is an example of fleeing from God and His commands (Jonah 1). God had told Jonah to go to Nineveh to preach, but Jonah did not want the people of Nineveh to be saved from God as they were cruel, wicked enemies of the Israelites. *"But Jonah arose to flee to Tarshish from the presence of the LORD"* (Jonah 1:3). Tarshish is in the opposite direction from Nineveh! Jonah did not want to follow God's command, so he hid from God. Of course, we know no one can hide from God. God caused a fish to swallow Jonah which gave Jonah time to rethink his plan!

We can be like Jonah and hide from God's commands. When we are told to teach others (Matt. 28:19), we claim inability or don't recognize our opportunities. That is hiding from God's commands. We are told to assemble with the saints (Heb. 10:25), but choose to go fishing or shopping instead. That is hiding from God's commands. God has told us to repent and be baptized (Acts 2:38), but we perceive ourselves as good enough without doing what God has asked. That is hiding from God's commands. God has told us what He wants us to do in the good news of the Bible and not obeying His gospel plan is hiding from God.

Don't think you can hide from God as He is an omnipresent and omniscient God. If you try to hide due to your sin or from His commandments, God is still calling you. Whether you respond "Polo" or not, God knows where you are, what you are, and what you are doing. No one can hide from God and He is calling for you!

Losing Your Kazip

My mother-in-law often says she has lost her kazip. She means she is older (almost 88 years old) without the energy and strength she used to have and so has lost her kazip. This is very frustrating to her, because she is proud of what she accomplished as a younger woman. Now she has to measure her activities as she tires very easily. However, she pushes to remain active in church, reads her Bible, and does other things she can do. In a recent newspaper article about her volunteer work, she was quoted as saying, "Always be the best you can be." If she doesn't try, she will never achieve anything and less kazip is not an excuse for not trying. My mother-in-law will tell you that anytime—any day.

Do we sometimes lose our kazip and forget to push on? Having no kazip can be our excuse for letting others do all the work. It has happened before and can happen to us, too! As Christians, we must do what we can and make every effort to work in God's kingdom. We cannot quit or wait for someone else to do what must be done. Jesus taught this in a parable frequently called the Parable of the Talents (Matt. 25:14-30). I like to call it the Parable of Doing What You Can. Jesus taught this parable during the last week of His life, because He was teaching and preaching to the very end.

In this parable, the master was traveling to a far country. He called three servants to him and gave each one coins weighed in an amount called a talent. A talent of silver would be worth about $400 thousand and a talent of gold about $6 million today. We don't know what type of coins was in the talents, just that the coins weighed a talent. Whether gold or silver, a talent of money is a lot to be responsible for!

The master gave the talents of money to the servants depending on their skills and abilities. The first received five talents of money, the second received two talents, and the third received one talent. Then the master went on his trip and after a period of time returned home. He called his servants to him to determine how they had managed his estate in his absence. The first and second servant had worked very hard doubling their money and had ten and four talents of money respectively to return to the master. He called them *good and faithful servants*. The third servant had hidden his money in a hole, which made the master MAD! This servant had made no effort to use the talents of money to increase the master's estate. The master called the third servant unprofitable, cast him into outer darkness, and gave his money to the first servant.

First, notice that the master knew each servant's skills and abilities and gave them the talents of money depending on what they could do. He knew the first servant had the most skills and abilities, the second next, and the third servant the least skills and abilities. He had given the most talents to the first, next to the second, and the least amount of money to the third, but expected all of them to work. He was very aware the third servant was the least gifted and expected more from the first and second servant. Still, He expected the third servant to work and to make a profit with his one talent of money. God always expects us to do what we can with the gifts He gives us.

Secondly, notice that the buried money was given to the first servant. This demonstrates a use-it-or-lose-it concept. For example, you studied piano until the sixth grade and never played again for the next thirty years. After thirty years, you will have lost the ability to play the piano: the use-it-or-lose-it concept. If you do not use the gifts God has given you, you will lose them. The third servant did not use his talent of money and so lost it. God always expects us to use our skills and abilities to do what we can in His kingdom.

Third, Jesus taught this parable during the week before His crucifixion. He knew exactly what would happen to Him in the next days, still he was teaching. Jesus was teaching, because He wanted *everyone* to know the truth. He was doing what He could while He was on earth. To follow Jesus' example, we must do what we can whenever we have opportunities and must also search for those opportunities.

So you can see whether you have lost your kazip or don't have a lot of skills and abilities, God expects everyone to work in His kingdom. He doesn't expect things you cannot do, because He knows what everyone is capable of doing. He does expect everyone to use what he has as he works. Hiding in a hole is not good for your ability or for you! Be like my mother-in-law and work as hard as you can for as long as you can. Use your skills and abilities to be a profitable servant for God.

Meandering Fences and Creeks

Recently my husband and I had a survey completed for a farm we were proposing to purchase. The survey narrative described one boundary as following a meandering fence. This boundary description meant the fence generally stayed on the boundary line, but was not exactly on it. Sometimes the fence wandered left and sometimes it wandered right of the surveyed line. When we questioned why the boundary line did not follow the perfectly good fence, the surveyor sagely advised us, "The boundary lines are always the boundary lines, but the fences come and go."

Several springs and creeks are on this same farm. Picture a creek as it meanders down the hill. The creek bubbles and dances as it flows through rocks and makes its crooked way down the hillside. A meandering creek is beautiful and offers quiet, restful settings as the water chooses the path of least resistance to make its path down the hill. The creek never flows uphill as it wanders through the farm and it always chooses the easiest path as it flows downward to join other creeks to make a bigger river with more impact of force and beauty.

Sometimes our Christian lives are like meandering fences and creeks. It is easy to stray from the narrow path the gospel has set for us and Jesus warns it is the harder path to follow. *"Because narrow is the gate and difficult is the way which leads to life, and there are few who find it"* (Matt. 7:14). Jesus knew we would have many influences and pressures in our lives which would push us right and left off the gospel path. Sometimes we are like the fence and generally follow the gospel path. After a quick misstep, we promptly regain the narrow path or we meander a little farther away and depend on our general sense of direction to find the path again. Sometimes we are like the creek and flow down the hill following the path of least resistance. These creek paths are pleasant, but also lead us away from the gospel path.

It is easy to be a meandering Christian and we might not even know it has happened to us. As the enthusiasm and excitement of learning the gospel decreases, the hum of daily living draws us back into old habits. Or new teachers teach a different way to live or to think of issues, which are more attractive or easier to implement than gospel Christianity. Wherever we are in our Christian lives, we must always check our path. Are we on the path leading to the narrow gate or have we meandered?

Paul's letter to the Galatians warned them of this same problem. *"I marvel that you are turning away so soon from Him who called you in the grace of Christ, to a different gospel, which is not another; but there are some who trouble you and want to pervert the gospel of Christ"* (Gal. 1:6-7). These Christians were like the meandering fence. They were listening to someone teaching a *perverted gospel*, something that wasn't Christ's gospel. This gospel might have been a little right or a little left of the line established by the true gospel or may have included some old habits. However, the true gospel is still the gospel no matter what these false teachers preach, just like the surveyor and the boundary line. It is important to each of us when we find our missteps to go back to the true gospel before we find ourselves on a totally different path. Just because someone teaches most of the Bible does not mean that it is Christ's gospel. True teachers do not add to or take away from the gospel. Diligent study is required of each individual to know for himself what the Bible teaches.

It is always easy to choose the easier path like the creek flowing downhill. Remember how the beautiful creek picks the path of least resistance to dance and to gurgle down the hill. It flows down shady groves, providing restful scenes with refreshing drink and joins other creeks to become a river with power and influence to the area. This type of meandering Christian enjoys the ease of being a creek and the authority of being part of a river. A comfortable life is a persuasive draw into this alternate gospel. In another of Paul's letters, he warns Christians about moving away from the gospel path and becoming like the meandering creek. *"And you, who once were alienated and enemies* in your mind by wicked works, yet now He has reconciled in the body of His flesh through death to present you holy, and blameless, and above reproach in His sight— if indeed you continue in the faith, grounded and steadfast, and are not moved away from the hope of the gospel which you heard" (Col. 1:21-23a).

It has always been easy to move away from the true gospel. False teachers sing a sweet song to entice us away. Some of these teachers don't even know they are teaching incorrectly and are sincerely teaching their beliefs. It is so easy to leave Christ's gospel.

Meandering Christians can be the most sincere people in the world as they live according to their version of the gospel. Sometime the rigor of study to learn what gospel is taught in the Bible is too difficult for individuals who find it is easier to go with the flow. Others know the gospel teaching and find themselves wandering from the path, because worldly enticements and old habits are strong influences. Still Christ's gospel message is the same for all and Paul's advice rings with truth and alarm. "Now this I say lest anyone should deceive you with persuasive words. . . . Beware lest anyone cheat you through philosophy and empty deceit, according to the tradition of men, according to the basic principles of the world, and not according to Christ" (Col. 2:4,8).

Christians must check their footsteps daily to ensure the gospel path is followed. No one else can do this for us nor do we want them to check for us. Each Christian is responsible for himself or herself and we cannot take the easy way or another's path. Personal study of the Bible is how we know the true gospel taught by Christ and preached by His disciples. Meandering is fine for fences and creeks, but not for Christians!

Are You A Gladiator?

Are you a gladiator? In Roman times, gladiators were a special sector of society. Most of them had the best training to sharpen their fighting skills and ate the best food to keep their bodies strong. The most elite of the gladiators became the darlings of Roman society and enjoyed all the offered privileges. Roman youths dreamed of being a famous gladiator with honor and prestige.

The kicker about being a gladiator was the job performance—gladiators fought to the death. Someone had to die each time there was a gladiator contest—maybe many people. The gladiator motto exemplified their lifestyle: "Eat, drink, and be merry; for tomorrow we die." They sought pleasure as a primary goal of their life. In their case, this attitude was because they expected a short life on earth with no better life afterward and did not know God. The gladiators chased pleasure anytime they could as that was the only reward they expected.

Luke 12:16-21 is a parable of a farmer who had a wonderful year with superior yield of all his crops. The farmer decided to build bigger barns to store the abundance. Then he said to himself, *"Soul, you have many goods laid up for many years; take your ease; eat, drink, and be merry."* The farmer thought he was self-sufficient and did not need anything from God. His reward for all his hard work was a comfortable life for the rest of his time on earth. Of course, that night, the rich farmer died and someone else had the benefit of all the crops stored in those bigger barns. This farmer chased comfort and pleasure. The reward he sought was stored in his barns to provide earthly comfort with no consideration for God's commandments.

It is a better plan to seek a reward in heaven. We can have pleasure on earth and live godly lives, too. In Ecclesiastes, Solomon assures us that finding pleasure while we live on earth is a good thing as long as we live as God has planned for us. In chapter 8:15, Solomon says, *"So I commend the enjoyment of life, because there is nothing better for a person under the sun than to eat and drink and be glad."* Solomon tells us we must follow God's commandments and work hard doing God's work to have our reward (9:1-12). Enjoying the pleasures of earth is part of a godly life. Some pleasures mentioned by Solomon are your work (2:24), your wealth (5:18-19), your good name (7:1), your life (9: 7-10), your spouse (9:9), and your youth (11:9). Solomon understood that prioritizing earthly pleasure over seeking God's pleasure is empty vanity and is no reward for man.

Enjoyment of life is a gift from God (Eccl. 3:13). The secret is to seek your reward with God in heaven, not here on earth. We must not be like the gladiators and seek our reward on earth, because such people do not know God or expect anything from Him. We must not be like the rich farmer depending on ourselves for our reward. We must be like the godly men Solomon describes in Ecclesiastes seeking God's pleasure first. It is good to enjoy life on earth as God made many beautiful things for us to use and appreciate. However, the things we chase must be God's commandments, not our pleasure and comfort. By putting God first, we will have our reward.

Solomon closes Ecclesiastes with these words: *"Let us hear the conclusion of the whole matter: Fear God and keep His commandments, For this is the whole duty of man"* (12:13). A home with God is our reward, not our life on earth.

Dear Diary

"Dear Diary, I am so glad you are here for me to talk through my problems. It is so helpful to have a sounding board for my thoughts and ideas and mainly my problems. I sure do wish you could really help me with my problems though. Some sound advice would really be cool. Diary, I am so glad I have you, but I sure do wish you could do more."

Diaries and blogs can be very important in an individual's life. The author knows the diary cannot provide advice and solve any problems for them, but is an outlet for expression of feelings, thoughts, and worries. With a blog, the author may even obtain comments from internet readers! However, neither of these outlets provides active help to the author. Even blog comments are just the reader's opinion, and not necessarily sound advice or real help.

I would like to suggest that prayers to God are better. God has already provided solid advice to us for daily living in our Bible. When we pray to God, He answers prayers. This is better than either a diary or a blog, because God loves us and is interested in each of us. God is particularly interested in listening to our problems and wants to help us with those problems. As we pray to God, we focus on the words we want to say and we try to be as specific as possible. The Holy Spirit even helps us to pray. *"Likewise the Spirit also helps in our weaknesses. For we do not know what we should pray for as we ought, but the Spirit Himself makes intercession for us with groanings which cannot be uttered"* (Rom. 8:26). Prayers to God result in good advice and answers.

The apostles watched Jesus as He continually prayed to God. Jesus frequently withdrew from the crowds and His apostles to spend time with God in prayer. They asked Him to teach them to pray (Luke 11:1-13) and He did. He taught them to pray earnestly for things important to them and others and praying to God is like a conversation with expectation of love and concern from God. Prayers are not memorized words you repeat mindlessly. A prayer to God should be about the things happening to you, about your worries, about your successes, about your plans, and about other people. In Colossians 4:2, Paul urges Christians to pray: *"Continue earnestly in prayer, being vigilant in it with thanksgiving"* and in Philippians 4:6, he writes, *"Be anxious for nothing, but in everything by prayer and supplication, with thanksgiving, let your requests be made known to God."*

We tell God what we want and need even though God already knows. God doesn't need to be told, but wants us to "talk" to Him—to be involved with Him. When God is part of your life, your anxiety about your problems is shared with God and your burden is lightened with our confidence in Him. You can be thankful for so many things God has already provided for you and the assurance He will continue to provide for you.

When we look at the verses where Jesus is teaching the apostles to pray, He teaches them to be persistent in prayers. If a father provides good things to his children, how much more will our heavenly Father give to those who ask? It is also important to work to make our prayers come true. If we pray to God for a job, then we must look for one. Our faith in God is demonstrated by our actions.

Prayer is not just a media for expressing our feelings and problems. It is an activity with participation from God, because God is active in prayers. God provides us both good advice and solutions to our problems and is involved in our daily lives. Diaries and blogs are nice, but God is essential!

"Just the facts, Ma'am"

How many are old enough to remember the television show *Dragnet*? When Sergeant Joe Friday was interviewing ladies, he would say "Just the facts, Ma'am, just the facts." He was not interested in their opinion or gossip, just wanted the facts related to the case. Knowing the facts is a good methodology for us as we make decisions in our everyday lives. This seemingly simple idea can save a lot of headache and heartache for all of us.

I bet Paul wished the first century Christians followed Sergeant Friday's methodology! In 2 Corinthians, Paul dealt with many false Corinthian accusations, because the Corinthians did not verify their facts. The Corinthians were listening to false teachers and believing everything they were told about Paul. For example, the false teachers were saying, Paul is wishy-washy (1:17), Paul preaches his own agenda (4:5), Paul does not walk his talk (10:10), Paul takes the credit of others' work (10:16), Paul is a poor speaker (11:6), Paul's work has no value because he works for free (11:7-9), and Paul does not love the Corinthians (11:11). Isn't this a weighty list? Clearly the Corinthians did not check their facts and took the words of others as true, so wrong conclusions were made. The Corinthians were allowing false teachers to spread lies about Paul, because that was easier than standing up for the truth or working to determine the truth.

The Corinthians needed to verify their facts and so do we. Sometimes it is easy for us to believe things just because we hear the "facts" a lot. For example, the above quote from Sergeant Friday is folklore and he never really said it! We hear that this quote was from the Dragnet show and believe it was really said on the show. Sergeant Friday would not have approved of our fact-finding!

An excellent example of fact-finders is the brethren living in Berea (Acts 17). After listening to Paul and Silas' lessons, the Bereans searched the Scriptures to ensure the lessons were true. This was their daily practice, not something they did on occasion. The Bereans checked their facts unlike many of the Corinthian brethren who believed the lies about Paul. These people were willing to do the hard work necessary to know what they believed and why they believed it. "Just the facts" could have been a Berean motto.

Today, we can be like either the Corinthians or the Bereans. It is as easy to believe lies today as it was for the Corinthians. Sometimes there is so much noise in our lives that we don't get to the important facts and don't make to the effort to get the facts either.

We often hear and read about people, our world, and our faith and the "facts" are not always true. Determining the truth of any situation is hard and frustrating work, but actions based on inaccurate information can lead to damaging consequences. In Matthew 27, Pilate knew Jesus was innocent and wanted to set Him free during the Passover feast. Pilate asked the crowd whom they would like to be freed—Jesus or Barabbas, a notorious murderer. The crowd had listened to their Jewish leaders and had been told what to believe about Jesus. They shouted for Barabbas to be released! These people had not checked their facts, but did as they were told. A murderer was freed and an innocent man was crucified.

Determining the facts of a situation has been important throughout time. In Deuteronomy 19:15, the Israelites were told to have two or more witnesses to ensure that the truth would be told. *"One witness shall not rise against a man concerning any iniquity or any sin that he commits; by the mouth of two or three witnesses the matter shall be established."* Paul reiterates this requirement in 2 Corinthians 13:1. The truth was so important that the old law required the witnesses to be the first to put their hands on anyone receiving a death penalty (Deut. 17:7) to be sure that the responsibility for truth was evident to all.

It is easy to go with the flow of popular facts. However, it is each individual's responsibility to check his facts and search for truth. Each person must be like the Bereans and Sergeant Friday and make decisions based on facts, not opinion or gossip. Then we can know that we have made the best decision that we could, because we had the facts!

Paul and the Thorn in His Flesh

Have you ever wondered about Paul and the thorn in his flesh? We know Paul had something that continually bothered him, a thorn, because Paul writes about it in 2 Corinthians 12:7-9: *"And lest I should be exalted above measure by the abundance of the revelations, a thorn in the flesh was given to me, a messenger of Satan to buffet me, lest I be exalted above measure. Concerning this thing I pleaded with the Lord three times that it might depart from me. And He said to me, 'My grace is sufficient for you, for My strength is made perfect in weakness.' Therefore most gladly I will rather boast in my infirmities, that the power of Christ may rest upon me."*

Most commentators think this thorn was some sort of physical ailment, especially poor eyesight. Poor eyesight is a possibility as in Galatians 4:15, Paul writes the Christians in Galatia *would have plucked out their own eyes and given them to me.* Paul was recalling how tenderly the Galatians had tended to him while he was sick and would have given him their own eyes. In Galatians 6:11, Paul mentioned that he is writing in large letters. If his handwriting was large so he could see it, then perhaps Paul's thorn was poor eyesight. We don't know for sure, but we do know it was a constant problem to him.

Okay, so maybe Paul could not see well. Is there anything special about that? Lots of people have poor eyesight or are blind. Did you ever wonder why no one healed Paul when lots of other people were healed by the apostles? Wonder why Paul didn't heal himself? Paul had even asked God three times to remove the thorn. Why would God want His apostle to have poor eyesight or some other physical infirmity? Wouldn't Paul have been more effective if he had a strong body that had been healed by a miracle from God?

Paul gave us the answer in the same verse. He had the thorn in his flesh to keep him from being exalted above measure or prideful. Paul was a man with a wonderful resume and many reasons to be proud of his accomplishments. He had been a leader among the Pharisees. He had an excellent education. He came from an influential and affluent family. He was a Roman citizen. He had a special revelation with Jesus on the road to Damascus and then other revelations from the Lord. He was widely traveled and known in many churches throughout the Roman Empire. Paul had many reasons to be especially proud of who he was and what he had accomplished!

Pride is one of the worst types of sin. Jesus lists pride along with murder, stealing, and wickedness as sins that come from a man's heart (Mark 7:20-22). In 1 John 2:15-17 John teaches us to put God over the things of this world. *"Do not love the world or the things in the world. If anyone loves the world, the love of the Father is not in him. For all that is in the world—the lust of the flesh, the lust of the eyes, and the pride of life—is not of the Father but is of the world. And the world is passing away, and the lust of it; but he who does the will of God abides forever."* Pride can get in anyone's way and block him from following the will of God.

Pride is why we depend on ourselves. We all applaud the self-made man and strive to be like him. As we face our daily problems, we often make our plans without praying or considering what God would want us to do. Maybe we pray about the big things, but the small things are just as important. When you habitually depend on yourself for the small things, it is not likely you will consider God on the big things. When we have the *pride of life*, we are depending on ourselves and not on God.

Modern science sometimes replaces God as man becomes prideful of his knowledge and accomplishments. We expect science to cure our diseases and to make our lives better. God did not promise either of these worldly desires and we shouldn't depend on science and technology instead of God. I don't mean that we should ignore scientific advancements or to shun it like some religious groups do, but we must not replace God with them.

Paul used this thorn to remind him to depend on the Lord. This thorn helped Paul to be humble. Note in verse 9, the Lord had told Paul

His grace was sufficient for him and His strength was made perfect in Paul's weakness. Paul was thankful for this reminder. He sums this up with these words. *"Therefore I take pleasure in infirmities, in reproaches, in needs, in persecutions, in distresses, for Christ's sake. For when I am weak, then I am strong"* (2 Cor. 12:10).

Paul's thorn is a lesson for us, too. If the Apostle Paul needed a thorn to remind him to not be prideful, then we must also guard ourselves from pride. Our accomplishments are pale compared to Paul's influence through the centuries. He guarded his heart from pride and we must guard our hearts, too.

Do As the Romans Do

I know you have heard one or both of these slogans – "What happens in Vegas, stays in Vegas" and "When in Rome, do as the Romans do." As we travel away from home, it is easy (and often encouraged) to let our hair down and let it all hang out. The lifestyle in Vegas and Rome is exotic and no one at home will ever know what happens there except for our pictures on Facebook. It is exciting to act a little bad (or maybe a lot bad) when no one will know. Besides, whom are we hurting when we take a vacation from God?

This attitude is wrong on so many levels. God must be part of our lives no matter where we happen to be, because He knows what we are doing anyway. However, I would like to explore only one point about letting your hair down when you are traveling. That point is going to a church assembly when you are not at home. I would like to suggest that attending church services at local congregations when you are traveling is a good idea and was practiced by the first century Christians.

In Hebrews 10:24-25, Paul writes, *"And let us consider one another in order to stir up love and good works, not forsaking the assembling of ourselves together, as is the manner of some, but exhorting one another."* This guidance would apply whether you were at home, Vegas, or Rome. You would be surprised at the brethren you will meet who have relatives and friends in your hometown. You might look around and see your next door neighbor or an old classmate! Not only is it a good practice to assemble with the brethren when you travel, but it is encouraging to the congregation you are visiting. Your faith is evident to the visited congregation and strengthens each one of them.

Not only does Paul instruct to us to assemble with one another, but he practiced what he preached. In Acts 20, Paul had been preaching in Greece for three months and was planning to return to Syria. He learned of a Jewish plot against him and decided to travel to Syria through Macedonia. This route was made partly by sea travel and they stopped at Troas where they stayed seven days. On the first day of the week, Paul and his group worshipped and had the Lord's Supper with the Troas Christians. I wonder if they delayed for seven days to have the Lord's Supper with the Troas brethren. Ships would have been leaving for Syria daily since Troas was a port city, but Paul lingered there.

Some of you might feel uncomfortable in a different congregation than in your hometown group. Well, I agree that some congregations are friendlier than others. My advice is to treat others as you would like to be treated. Oh yes, that is the golden rule you were taught as a child! Whether you are the visitor or the host Christian, greet other brethren assembling to worship God. All of us should be glad others have made God their priority and have come to worship. Remember, each of us is important to God and we should make each Christian feel important to us. This is part of *exhorting one another*. When we strive to be an encouragement to other Christians, we are living as the first century Christians did.

Are you ready to go to Rome with me? Paul was a Roman citizen—let's do as Paul did. Paul was in Rome as a prisoner during some of the last years of his life. Sometimes he was under house arrest and sometimes he was in a dungeon. While in Rome, Paul taught Roman guards and anyone else who would listen, wrote the four prison epistles (Ephesians, Colossians, Philippians, and Philemon), and was an encouragement to Christians everywhere. As Paul was brought to Rome, he was often in chains, was shipwrecked, and was bitten by a viper. Still, he worshipped God, taught others, and was an encouragement to all Christians. Can you imagine being chained to Paul in Rome? Let's go to Rome and be like Paul by worshipping God while we are there! Then we are doing as the Romans do!

The Third Son

Jesus taught with so many parables! Some of them are only one or two verses long, but the depth of meaning is fantastic. I am sure He would often look around the countryside for inspiration to make His point. For example, in the parable about the sower and the seed (Matt. 13:1-9), Jesus was teaching the crowd from a boat. It is possible Jesus saw someone in a field sowing seed and used that visual to teach. Even if there was no sower at that moment, the whole crowd was familiar with sowing seeds in their agrarian society. So Jesus used what they knew to teach them something they did not know. Or maybe He would make His point by describing a scene they all wished could happen, such as finding a hidden treasure in a field (Matt. 13:44).

In Matthew 21:23-32, Jesus was being challenged by the chief priests and elders of the temple about His authority and so He told them a parable about the authority of a father and his sons. *"A man had two sons, and he came to the first and said, 'Son, go, work today in my vineyard.' He answered and said, 'I will not,' but afterward he regretted it and went. Then he came to the second and said likewise. And he answered and said, 'I go, sir,' but he did not go. Which of the two did the will of his father? They said to Him, 'The first'"* (21:28-31).

Jesus taught this parable to show the chief priests and temple elders that they were like the second son, the son who did not do as his father had requested. The sinners whom the priests and elders considered beneath them had repented, were doing as the father had requested, and were the first son. The chief priests and temple elders definitely did not like being portrayed as a disobedient son and sought to *lay hands on Him*. They understood Jesus meant they were disobedient and two-faced to God in this parable and did not like it at all!

Let's look at this parable a different way and see if we can learn something to help us be better Christians. The first son would not obey the father when initially asked, but finally did as the father requested. In the end, he did the right thing by working in the vineyard, but wanted to do it when he was ready. This son wanted to be considered a good son by his father, but do his own thing also. He was like all the good people we know who are not members of God's church. These good people would rather do their plans first, then do whatever God wants—if they have the time. These good people feel this is all they need to do, since they are not a bad son and will eventually do as the father asks.

The second son told the father he would go work in the vineyard, but did not go. We all know this type of person, too—the kind of person who doesn't practice what they preach or a two-faced hypocrite. Church pews often have hypocrites in them. A common complaint is the businessman at church on Sunday and cheating on Monday. This "son" is the excuse many people use for not going to church at all and gives Christians a bad reputation. No one likes the hypocritical second son.

We need to be like the third son! I know a third son is not in the parable, but the part about a third son could go like this. The father asks the third son to go work in the vineyard. The third son tells the father, "I go, sir," and then immediately goes to work in the vineyard. This son does as his father asks and does it when the father asks. He is a good son doing the father's work in the manner the father has asked. This son walks his talk, is not a hypocrite, and is an obedient son. Striving to be like the third son should be every Christian's goal!

Your Household Idols

Aren't we lucky we don't live in the days of idol worship? My husband and I have visited the ruins of Chichen Itza in Mexico. We climbed the staircase of the El Castillo pyramid which is a temple to the Mayan god, *Kukulkan* (a Maya feathered serpent deity). Our guide told us the priests pulled the heart out of a live person to offer as a sacrifice at the top of the pyramid. This heart was laid in a bowl sitting on the belly of a reclining stone idol. Its chiseled face blankly watched as the heart was set on fire and the person died.

All ancient idols weren't so dramatic and demanding. For example, ancient Haran families often had household idols. These idols were figurines displayed on a shelf or table in the house and important to a particular family or person. This was probably the type of idol mentioned in Genesis 31 which is the story of Rachel and Jacob fleeing from Rachel's father, Laban.

Jacob had worked for Laban for fourteen years to earn the bride price for Rachel and Leah and then six more years for wages. During these last six years, Laban had changed Jacob's wages ten times to continually have the most advantage over Jacob. However, God blessed Jacob during those years. If Jacob's wages were spotted sheep, then many new lambs had spots. If dark goats were Jacob's wages, then new kids were dark. Laban became unsettled as Jacob was becoming more prosperous than he.

Jacob realized Laban would always look out for number one and was told by God to return home with his family, servants, and livestock. This is where the household idols come into the story. Jacob asked his two wives if they would leave with him. They responded, *"Are we not considered strangers by him? For he has sold us and also completely con-*

sumed our money." When Rachel was packing her belongings for the trip, she packed the household idols belonging to her father. We don't know if Rachel worshipped these idols or just took them for revenge on her father. After all, her father tricked Jacob into marrying Leah instead of her for his first wife and spent all the bride price. All we know is she took them.

Laban was mad when he found Jacob and his household had left. However, he was outraged to find the household idols were gone! He demanded the return of the idols when he caught up with Jacob. Jacob denied having the idols and promised the death of anyone found with them. Rachel had hidden the idols in her camel saddle and sat on it during the search. She claimed her "monthlies" and was left alone on the saddle. The idols were not found and Laban returned home without them. We don't know what she did with those little statues, but she kept them that day!

The reason for telling the story about Rachel and her idols is to show that idols can be important only to the worshipper. Something that is significant to you can become your idol. A big house with a manicured lawn may be your idol, if that is the priority of your life. High fashion and good looks may be your idol, if all your time and energy are spent there. Public service may be your idol, if done for personal recognition, power, or money. Your household idol is whatever is most important to you and can be something you are very comfortable with. Nothing as scary as *Kukulkan* is required. Money and prestige usually top the list of possible idols and are not unique to our society.

The Bible warns us we cannot serve God and riches—for we will love one and hate the other (Matt. 6:24). Of course, we need money for food, clothing and shelter, but are we good stewards of the money God has given us? When money is used only to grow your bank account, you are not serving God first; money has become your household idol.

Prestige is your idol when your actions are calculated to make yourself more important. When your good works are designed to be applauded by people, then those are not good works done to please God. Prestige is its own reward. In Jesus' parable about the Pharisee praying aloud in the temple (Luke 18:9-14), He taught that the approval of the watching people was the only reward for that prayer. In another lesson (Matt. 6:16-17), Jesus said men who walked around with disfigured faces to appear to others as if they had been fasting were hypocrites. *"Assuredly, I say to you, they have their reward"* was Jesus' statement about those men! Don't worship prestige and seek approval of other men instead of God's approval. This prestige is a stone idol just like Kukulkan!

We don't live in a time when Kukulkan is an entity to be feared, but this doesn't mean we aren't susceptible to idol worship. Study your priorities. Be sure that your time and energy are spent serving our living God, not your household idol.

Looking Into the Abyss

While we are living our pleasant lives, do we dread the abyss, the hard thing requiring a strong faith? We worry about an awful disease taking slow, painful control of our lives or the lives of those we love. We worry about financial stability for ourselves and our families. We worry about worldwide conflict filled with hatred and violence shaping how we live. We worry about random, individual acts of violence destroying the fabric of our families like the Columbine High School shooting. As Christians, sometimes we worry about our faith remaining strong when we face our dark abyss whose yawn sucks us into its deepest craters filled with pain and uncertainty.

We know people whose faith is strong during their hard time and those who crumble. There is an inspiring story of faith from the Columbine shooting[7] – the girl who said, "yes." One of the gunman asked a girl (could have been one of two young ladies), "Do you believe in God?" and shot her when she said, "yes." All of us hope to be like that young lady, but are afraid of such a test.

Christians have big shoes to follow which show us how to be faithful as we stand at our abyss. We know the first century Christians were beaten, tortured, and killed for their faith. They knew their faith would immediately be tested by the Roman and Jewish authorities. There was no uncertainty about that. Do we dread a similar testing of our faith? Apostle Peter reassured them with these words: *"In this you greatly rejoice, though now for a little while, if need be, you have been grieved by various trials, that the genuineness of your faith, being much more precious than gold that perishes, though it is tested by fire, may be found to praise, honor, and glory at the revelation of Jesus Christ, whom having not seen you love. Though now you do not see Him, yet believing, you*

---
[7] Cassie Rene Bernal, 04/12/2012, *http://acolumbinesite.com/victim/cassie.html.*.

rejoice with joy inexpressible and full of glory, receiving the end of your faith—the salvation of your souls" (1 Pet. 1:6-9). We can be as faithful as these Christians by leaning on God during our hard times which test our faith. Our faith is supported by our certain hope of eternal salvation with God.

We don't doubt God is there as we look into our abyss, but we are afraid our strength and faith will not endure the test. This is a multi-faceted problem, but Apostle Paul describes methods for strengthening and maintaining our faith as the armor of faith. *"Finally, my brethren, be strong in the Lord and in the power of His might. Put on the whole armor of God, that you may be able to stand against the wiles of the devil. For we do not wrestle against flesh and blood, but against principalities, against powers, against the rulers of the darkness of this age, against spiritual hosts of wickedness in the heavenly places. Therefore take up the whole armor of God, that you may be able to withstand in the evil day, and having done all, to stand. Stand therefore, having girded your waist with truth, having put on the breastplate of righteousness, and having shod your feet with the preparation of the gospel of peace; above all, taking the shield of faith with which you will be able to quench all the fiery darts of the wicked one. And take the helmet of salvation, and the sword of the Spirit, which is the word of God; praying always with all prayer and supplication in the Spirit, being watchful to this end with all perseverance and supplication for all the saints"* (Eph. 6:10-18).

The armor of God supports us and our hope as we stand at our abyss. Truth, righteousness, the gospel of peace, faith, salvation, and the Spirit are our armor and our weapons. We can win against any abyss armed with such strong armor and supported by our hope of heaven and prayer. The knowledge of God's love for us and His presence with us during dark times comforts and supports us. Our faith during our dark time can become an example to others which is a double win!

Sometimes we cannot help but dread the unknown. However, our greatest joy is knowing that God is there as we approach a chasm in our life. Maintaining our armor and sharpening our weapons is the best way to be ready. We do this by daily studying God's word, praying to God, and ensuring our walk follows His path. A good soldier pays attention to his armor and weapons to be ready for battle and this is how we ready ourselves for an abyss.

Girding your waist with truth is knowledge of God's word and the first step for maintaining our armor. Filling our hearts with the truth of God gives us strength and supports us in our trials. This foundation is the beginning and basic element of our hope in God and His protection.

The breastplate of righteousness is our moral goodness as we live in the truth of God. Remember the Roman soldier wearing his breastplate across his chest to protect his heart? Our heart is righteous as we follow God's commandments and our righteousness protects us when we are looking into an abyss.

When we are shod with the gospel of peace, it means we are prepared to fight for and defend our faith. A true soldier cannot be prepared for a fight when he is barefoot. Again, knowing the gospel and making it a part of your heart prepares a Christian. Our knowledge of the truth and our righteous heart prepares us to fight even when dark times come.

The shield of faith is our trust in the word of God. The Bible tells us that faith comes from hearing the word of God. We know the truth of the word and have faith God will do all He has promised. Our faith shelters us as a safe harbor in a storm just like ships are sheltered in the safe harbor. The waves buffet the ship which rides the waves holding to its anchor of faith.

The helmet of salvation is the assurance that God has forgiven our sins and promised eternal life in heaven with Him. The helmet protects our head and our thoughts, because we know our salvation is guaranteed. When we are sure of our salvation, we can handle the hard times that are part of life. To effectively wear the helmet of salvation, a good Christian soldier centers his thoughts on God.

The sword of the Spirit is the word of God and our offensive weapon. The word of God or the Spirit is with us all day, every day. Using the sword of the Spirit, we learn to depend on God, not ourselves or others, during our hard times and the good times of our life. Actively and effectively using our sword protects us in our daily battles.

Our whole armor of faith is supported by prayer. Paul told the Ephesians to pray always. Praying to God keeps us thoughtful of God's word and our need for God. Prayer helps us to remain close in God's care, to not become distracted by our earthly cares, and is essential during our dark times.

Paul prayed for the Ephesian Christians' strength as they faced their trials. *"For this reason I bow my knees to the Father of our Lord Jesus Christ, from whom the whole family in heaven and earth is named, that He would grant you, according to the riches of His glory, to be strengthened with might through His Spirit in the inner man"* (Eph. 3:14-16). This prayer is also for us today!

We all dread the abyss. However, when we daily maintain our armor of God, we are prepared and can overcome all doubts and uncertainties. After all, we have God on our side!

The Elephant in the Room

Have you ever been mad at a member of your family and said things you wished you hadn't? After the argument is over, those words hang around like an elephant in the room. Everyone involved in the argument remembers the words when the emotion of the argument is over and issues are smoothed out. Don't you wish you had listened to Solomon's advice in Proverbs 21:23? *"Whoever guards his mouth and tongue keeps his soul from troubles."* With good advice like that, elephants would never be in the room!

It is so easy to speak mean, angry words without thinking of the consequences. Each word shoots like a bullet from your mouth to hurt and maim the people we love. Spoken words cannot be swallowed as only unspoken words have that feature. Then, each mean, angry spoken word grows into the elephant in the room.

Solomon writes a lot in the book of Proverbs about controlling our words. He warns us of angry words, gossiping words, lying words, and all types of words that cause harm. A good example of his advice is Proverbs 15:28. *"The heart of the righteous studies how to answer, but the mouth of the wicked pours forth evil."* James also warned us about speech without thought. *"The tongue is a fire, a world of iniquity"* (3:6). We must *think* before we speak! I know this seems obvious, but it can be hard to do.

Sometimes our words are thrown out thoughtlessly to avoid a hard situation or to protect ourselves. Remember how Peter denied Jesus three times before the rooster crowed? I know a rooster isn't an elephant, but Peter knew his words were wrong. Jesus emphasized this when He stared at Peter after his third denial. Jesus had warned Peter he would do this earlier that night, but still, Peter could not control his tongue. Peter was not thinking before he spoke in this tense, volatile situation at the house of the high priest. Peter's words were thoughtless, lying words when he claimed he did not know Jesus to protect himself.

Maybe instead of fixating on what not to say, we should concentrate on what we should say. Solomon tells us, *"A man has joy by the answer of his mouth, and a word spoken in due season, how good it is!"* (Prov. 15:23). Even in hard situations, our words must be thoughtful, uplifting, and truthful. Notice Solomon talks about words spoken in due season, meaning that sometimes we should be quiet and keep our words to ourselves. When we are arguing with those we love, thoughtful words are the best words. Truthful words can be delivered with a soft answer (Prov. 15:1a) or as a burning fire (Prov. 16:27). Both ways may be truthful, but truth delivered in the harshest manner grows into an elephant in the room to hurt those we love.

Controlling our words is an important part of being a Christian. *"If anyone among you thinks he is religious, and does not bridle his tongue but deceives his own heart, this one's religion is useless"* (James 1:26). Our words have a lasting impact. Our children will remember the Bible lessons they were taught or the denigrations they endured. Our spouse will remember that we loved them or we found no value in them. Our neighbor will see what Christianity means or will find hypocrisy next door. Our work associates will see a Christian with honesty and integrity or a backbiting, ladder-climbing scoundrel. The bag boy at the grocery store will see a Christian example or a whining person to avoid. The difference can be our words. *"Out of the same mouth proceed blessing and cursing. My brethren, these things ought not to be so"* (James 3:10).

Words are important. Words can hurt or help, be truth or lies. The choice belongs to each of us as only we can choose our words. It is a daily battle to control our words, but we must prevail. Arguments can be constructive, but anger during our arguments can make our words cruel. It is hard to control our words when we feel threatened or angry, but this is the most important time. Consider your words carefully to avoid an elephant in the room!

My Friend

Let me tell you about my friend, Andy, who was a thirty-something young man with his life ahead of him. He had a career, a beautiful home, everything—until he found out about the cancer. Yes, Andy had everything, including a disease that would kill him in a few months. However, Andy had something else, too. He had God and had been a Christian for many years. The thing I want to tell you about my friend Andy is that he had a working faith and demonstrated his faith by his works. While Andy was dying, he was writing encouraging letters to other Christians and I was one of those recipients. He knew I was struggling with a hard time in my life and wanted to encourage me to stay the course and have faith in God.

In James 2 the writer tells us, *"I will show you my faith by my works"* and *"faith without works is dead"* (vv. 18, 26). Genuine faith changes us and is evident in our lives. When we believe and want to be as God wants us to be, our faith and our works naturally complement each other. Faith and works are not mutually exclusive and we don't get a pass because we are dying, old, sick, or for any other reason. We must demonstrate our faith with our works.

Works are a natural outcome of saving faith. A person saying he or she has faith with ruthless business practices does not have genuine faith. A faithful businessman cannot lie, cheat, and steal in the office and worship sincerely on Sunday. This is hypocrisy, not faith. At the same time, a faithful person with strong belief cannot wait for someone else to perform good works. "As we have opportunity, we must teach others and do good deeds" (Gal. 6:10).

Sometimes our faith is most evident when life is hard. People can be kind when they have everything they could want. It is not a stretch to give our old clothes to Goodwill. After all, we don't want them anymore and have plenty of other clothes. What if you only had the clothes you were wearing? Would you still share your clothing with someone else? Could you be like the widow who gave two small coins to the temple treasury (Mark 12:41-44)? Those coins were all the widow had and she probably did not eat that day after giving them to the temple. This widow's faith was evident by her works and Jesus valued her donation more than any other.

Paul's faith was evident by his works during his second Roman imprisonment. This imprisonment was very different from Paul's first imprisonment of house arrest. At this time, Nero was blaming Christians for the fire which had destroyed half of Rome and was persecuting them with extreme cruelty. Paul was in a Roman cell without hope of release and facing probable death. Paul's active faith was demonstrated as he wrote a letter, which we know as 2 Timothy, to a young preacher. In this letter, Paul encouraged his young protégée to remain faithful and gave him final words of encouragement. Paul knew his life would soon end at the hands of Nero, however; he continued encouraging those around him and those he loved. Until his life was over, Paul was preaching and teaching others about the gospel. Can't you see Paul's faith by his works?

My friend knew that his body was dying, but his faith was still strong and very much alive. Andy was following the example of Apostle Paul and the widow. He was working and showing others what a strong faith should look like and he didn't stop when the work was hard.

The outcome of our faith is our works. How can anyone know you are a Christian if there is no evidence? Sometimes the work is small like the widow's coins. Sometimes the work is a letter like Andy's or Paul's. Don't think your work is too small or you have done enough. How can you know the lasting impact of your work? Look for your opportunities and go and do them. You get better with practice and strengthen your faith as you work. Then, you will be showing your faith by your works!

Peter and Geometry

I don't know how well you scored in mathematics in school, but the Apostle Peter had a basic knowledge of geometry! I know geometry is an odd way to demonstrate Biblical principles; however, this model can show us how Peter taught the entire gospel message. So how did Peter apply geometry to teach us the gospel?

The basic element of geometry is a point which is a fundamental object conforming to certain truths. Peter's points described basic truths relating to faith. Three points define a plane which is two-dimensional object. Peter used three faith-based points to define his first two-dimensional Faith Plane. Two intersecting planes define a three-dimensional space. By adding a fourth faith-based point to define an intersecting faith plane, Peter established his three-dimensional Gospel Space. Peter then applied time to his Gospel Space to have four dimensions!

Peter's **first point** or fundamental truth was the church is built on faith in God and Christ. In the book of Matthew, Jesus and His apostles had been teaching and performing many miracles throughout Galilee. The multitudes of people had *"marveled when they saw the mute speaking, the maimed made whole, the lame walking, and the blind seeing; and they glorified the God of Israel"* (Matt. 15:31). Of course, the Pharisees and chief priests did not like Jesus' popularity and were constantly trying to prove Jesus was not from God. The environment for Jesus and His apostles was divided with the people clamoring for more teaching and miracles, while the Pharisees and chief priests worked hard to obstruct Jesus.

In this contentious atmosphere, Jesus asked His apostles who the people said He was (Matt. 16:13-20). The apostles repeated some ideas they had heard from the people, but Jesus' important question came next. *"But who do you say that I am?"* (16:15). Peter answered Jesus, *"You are the Christ, the Son of the living God"* (16:16). Jesus affirmed this knowledge was from God and this statement of faith was the rock on which He would build His church. *So Peter defined his first point – the church is built on faith in God and Jesus Christ.*

Peter's **second point** or fundamental truth was faith requires repentance and baptism to be saved. In Acts 2, the apostles *"were all with one accord in one place. And suddenly there came a sound from heaven, as of a rushing mighty wind, and it filled the whole house where they were sitting. Then there appeared to them divided tongues, as of fire, and one sat upon each of them. And they were all filled with the Holy Spirit and began to speak with other tongues, as the Spirit gave them utterance"* (2:1-4). Then, Peter preached a sermon about the good news of Jesus and the gospel to the assembled Jews gathered in Jerusalem from all over the known world for Pentecost. Those Jews were convinced Jesus was Lord and Christ and had been crucified for their sins. Stricken to their hearts, they asked Peter what to do. Peter told them, *"Repent, and let every one of you be baptized in the name of Jesus Christ for the remission of sins; and you shall receive the gift of the Holy Spirit"* (2:38). Three thousand souls were baptized that day! *Here Peter defined his second point by teaching faith requires repentance and baptism to be saved.*

Peter's **third point** or fundamental truth was faith and the gospel are for both Jew and Gentile. Acts 10 has the story about a Gentile centurion named Cornelius who was a devout man, prayed to God always, and had taught his household to fear God (Acts 10:1-2). Cornelius had a vision from God which told him to send for Peter. Meanwhile, Peter had his own vision from God which told him that nothing God had made was unclean (including the Gentiles). After arriving at Cornelius' house, Peter taught Cornelius and his household about Jesus and the gospel. While Peter preached to these Gentiles, *"the Holy Spirit fell upon all those who heard the word"* (10:44) just as it had on the apostles and Jewish believers in Acts 2. The Gentiles could also *"speak with tongues and magnify God"* just as the Jewish believers could do. Those Gentiles believed and were baptized! *This made Peter's third point –faith and the Gospel are for both Jew and Gentile.*

Peter's three faith-based points or fundamental truths demonstrated that the church is built on faith, faith requires repentance and baptism, and faith is for everyone which fully defines *Peter's first two-dimensional Faith Plane.*

Peter **fourth point** or fundamental truth was faith required obedience of God over man. In Acts 4, Peter and John had been put in prison by the Jewish Sanhedrin counsel for preaching about Jesus and the gospel. The Sanhedrin had let them go after ordering them not to preach in the name of Jesus. Of course, all the apostles continued preaching and added more people to the church daily. Peter and the other apostles were imprisoned and brought before the council again where they were denounced for preaching the gospel. In Acts 5:29, Peter's reply is, "We ought to obey God rather than men" and preached to the council! After being beaten for their preaching, Peter and the apostles rejoiced, because they were worthy to suffer for Jesus' name! *Peter's fourth point or fundamental truth was faith requires obedience of God's commandments over man's rules.*

This fourth point or fundamental truth blended perfectly with Peter's first three faith-based points creating a second Faith Plan to define Peter's **three-dimensional Gospel Space.** His Gospel Space shows the church is built on faith in God and Jesus Christ, faith requires repentance and baptism to be saved, faith and the gospel are for everyone, and faith requires obedience to God.

Peter added time, the **fourth dimension**, to his Gospel Space. Peter taught that Jesus was eternal, because He was alive in the past, present, and future which confirmed the gospel message. Here are some time-based points established by Peter.

For Peter's **past-time** point, let's consider two of Peter's writings. Peter affirmed Jesus during Noah's time in 1 Peter 3:18-20 when Peter told us Jesus preached through Noah to the people of that day. Peter also affirmed Jesus is the Christ as foretold by the prophets throughout the ancient days (2 Pet. 1:19-20). With these two examples, Peter demonstrated Jesus existed in the past.

There are so MANY choices to demonstrate Peter's **current-time** point, because the four gospels (Matthew, Mark, Luke, and John) have many narratives of Peter and Jesus. For one account, in Matthew 14:22-33, the apostles sailed across the Sea of Galilee while Jesus stayed behind to pray. A great storm arose and the apostles were sure the boat would sink. Suddenly, they thought a ghost was walking across the storm's waves before realizing it was Jesus! Peter said, *"Lord, if it is You, command me to come to You on the water."* While Peter focused on Jesus, he got out of the boat and walked toward Jesus. Suddenly, Peter realized he was doing the impossible and began to sink! Jesus helped Peter back to the boat while all the apostles in the boat said, *"Truly You are the Son of God."*

Another story of Peter and Jesus emphasized Jesus' resurrection from the dead to solidify our current-time point. After Jesus' crucifixion, Peter and most of the apostles were together in a closed room (John 20). Jesus had been buried in a tomb for three days and there were stories of His resurrection. Suddenly Jesus was in the room with them – alive and well! Jesus had risen from the dead and was with Peter and the other apostles! What a wonderful current-time point!

Peter showed us with these current-time points that Jesus was alive at the same time as Peter and had risen from the dead. There are many wonderful examples to make current-time points of Peter and Jesus. Rather than repeat the entire gospel here, let these two stories of Jesus and Peter establish our current-time point.

This leaves only the **future-time** point to fully demonstrate a gospel timeline with a past, present and future. Peter handled this well by showing us that Jesus is in heaven! The final time Peter saw Jesus was when Jesus ascended into heaven (Acts 1:9-11). Peter watched as Jesus *was taken up and a cloud received Him out of their sight* and two angels told him Jesus would return in like manner! Peter told us this same thing again in 2 Peter 3:10: *"But the day of the Lord will come as a thief in the night, in which the heavens will pass away with a great noise, and the elements will melt with fervent heat; both the earth and the works that are in it will be burned up."* Peter wanted everyone to be ready for the coming of our Lord Jesus and this established our future-time point.

In these time-point stories, Peter demonstrated that Jesus was alive in the past, walked with Peter on earth, and is now in heaven for the future, which established time, the fourth dimension, for his Gospel Space.

Peter was good with geometry. His four-dimensional model demonstrated that Jesus is eternal, the gospel plan is for everyone, the church is built on faith, and faith requires repentance, baptism, and obedience. Peter would have done well on geometry tests!

www.ingramcontent.com/pod-product-compliance
Lightning Source LLC
Chambersburg PA
CBHW061336040426
42444CB00011B/2949